My Cup Runneth Over

Regina Miller Sanders

DEDICATION

I would like to dedicate this book to all who have been diagnosed with any kind of cancer and to their families and friends. It seems you have been thrust into the valley of the shadow of death, but when you come out of that valley your cup will overflow with joy unspeakable! Surely goodness and mercy follow you all the days of your life!

CONTENTS

ACKNOWLEDGMENTS

I would like to first and foremost that God for walking through the valley of the shadow of death with me. I thank Him for His presence, for His rod and staff which brought me comfort in this frightening time in my life.

I thank my family: my husband who stood strongly by my side when I was at my weakest. I thank my daughters, who are truly women of valor, for showing courage in some of the hardest moments of our lives. I thank my parents for their strength, encouragement, love, and acts of kindness expressed to me. I thank the many churches who have kept me lifted in prayer continuously. And I thank you, the readers for your support by purchasing this book.

The Lord bless you and keep you and make His face to shine upon you and surround you with His favor like a shield and bring you peace which surpasses all understanding.

1 OVERCOMING THE ADVERSARY

Revelation 12:11a, "And they overcame him (the adversary because of the blood of the Lamb and because of the word of their testimony."

I am here with you today to help you overcome the adversary that is reaching out attempting to devour you and your family. It is my prayer that something you hear in my testimony adds arsenal to your warfare to overcome the adversary.

I am especially excited about being here tonight, this night in particular, as it marks the beginning of Passover, the Lord's Spring Feast. When I think of being made in God's image, I think of Him, yes as the Spirit He is, but also with a body like ours. Passover, to me, represents the arm of the Lord.

Exodus 6:6, "Therefore say to the children of Israel: "I AM the LORD; I will bring you out from under the burdens of the Egyptians, I will rescue you from their bondage, and I will redeem you with an outstretched arm and with great judgments."

Tonight, I believe, is the night that many will be brought out from under the burdens of the Egyptians (mitzrayim: narrow places, lack, captivity), cancer, or whatever ailment you have been diagnosed with, and will be rescued from your bondage. Tonight, He is going to redeem you with an outstretched arm. How would you respond if you heard Jesus ask you to meet Him at a certain time and place so He could reward you with incredible miracles and breakthroughs in your life? It's not by coincidence or accident that you are here, but by divine appointment, tonight is that appointment.

Passover is a prophetic picture of God's only Son, Jesus Christ, who would one day come into the world to give His life on a cross to forgive your sins and mine, and bring healing and prosperity. John 1:29 declares,

"Behold the Lamb of God who takes away the sins of the world."
In John 10:10 Jesus tells us, "The thief comes ONLY to STEAL and KILL and DESTROY; I came that they (YOU) may have LIFE, and have it ABUNDANTLY."

January 2016, I was a blessed woman. I had been healed of introversion. I was teaching a group on Facebook about coming out of their shell of introversion, and I was writing a book on this same topic. I was posting weekly Biblical teachings on YouTube, and then, God blessed me more with a weekly satellite radio broadcast allowing my voice to be heard in places such as Hong Kong, Germany, and Canada. I never would have been heard in these places without God. It's not about me, it's about Him! When I say He gave me a broadcast, I mean, He literally gave it to me free of charge from January through April. My husband and I had prayed and decided to keep the radio ministry going after the free time. We were blessing others and we were being blessed by them each time they shared a testimony with us. Now, you know the enemy does not like it when you are blessing others or when you are being blessed and he is going to go into action to stop you anyway he possibly can. And that's what happened; an attack from the enemy!

The unthinkable happened on May 5, 2016. I started having severe abdominal pain. Initially, I refused to go to the hospital because the next day, May 6, 2016, my daughter, who was in cosmetology school, was participating in a fashion show to raise money for domestic violence awareness and victims, and I was one of her models. The day of the fashion show the pain was even worse! I was bloated so much I didn't know if I could still fit into my dress. I purchased a corset to hold everything in. I would not tell anyone that I was in this excruciating pain. I was determined to get through this night. This was HER night to shine. I prayed, "Lord, please don't let me pass out as I walk down the runway." Praise the Lord, He heard my prayer and answered. I didn't pass out and no one figured out that I was in this pain until after the event when I told them.

Once my family discovered I was in such severe pain they tried to get me to go to the ER but at this point, I was exhausted and just wanted to go to bed. I agreed to go to ER the next day if I was still experiencing the pain. May 7, 2016 the pain was unbearable. On a scale of zero to 10, it was a 50! I did not put off a trip to the ER any longer; I could no longer take the severity of the pain. I chose to go to the ER which was in the same city as my daughter's school. Leaning into my own understanding, I thought it would be more convenient for my family if I had to be admitted. Now, we all know that Scripture instructs us NOT to lean into our own understanding, and through this, I learned why! How many of you know that convenience is not always best. The staff at the ER got me back for evaluation rather quickly because I told them I thought I had an intestinal blockage. The doctor ordered a CT scan and discovered a mass on my colon. He then sent me home with a prescription for pain medication, instructed me to buy a laxative, and provided me with the phone number for an associate to call on Monday (this was Saturday) and schedule a colonoscopy.

I followed his instructions to the T. I struggled through the weekend with excruciating pain which the medication did not help. The laxative…well, it made me vomit. (I apologize for the gruesome details, but I am being completely honest with you.) Finally Monday arrived. I phoned the physician's office to schedule the colonoscopy as instructed. He had a very nice appointment scheduler who said in the kindest voice, "We can get you in for a colonoscopy on May 23rd at such and such time…" I simply replied, "Thank you, but if I wait until May 23rd I will be dead!!!"

Once my husband returned home from work I told him how it went with attempting to get an appointment for a colonoscopy. He decided we were going back to the ER because my pain levels were still so high and NOTHING they instructed me to do was helping. Once again, leaning into my own understanding (which doesn't work) I had him take me back to the same ER so it would be convenient for the family if I was admitted. In my mind, and what seemed logical, they already had the CT results showing a mass on my colon, surely they would admit me to see what was going on; if nothing else, they would go on and do an emergency colonoscopy and decide if I needed to be admitted. Isn't that what they do at the emergency room when they detect an abnormality on you colon? Not at this hospital! I believed with all my heart that they would help me. I just needed and wanted someone to really listen to what I was saying and HELP ME! At this time, they attempted an enema and I thought they would kill me before they completed the process, which by the way, was UNSUCCESSFUL! They said, "The impaction is just too high up for us to reach it." They then brought me discharge papers and another prescription for pain medication. They sent me home with apologies.

I suffered through the next few days convinced that no one was going to help me. I was refusing to return to ANY emergency department, convinced they were all going to be the same way. However, the following Thursday night, my pain levels were still through the roof and my blood pressure had risen to dangerously high levels. My husband had been up since 4:00 AM working, so I called my mother and asked her to drive me back to the emergency room. When she came to pick me up my husband gave her strict and specific instructions: "Do NOT take her back to the same ER she has been going to. I do not care how much she protests. Take her ANYWHERE but there. When you get to the ER tell them she is

NOT coming home until they KNOW what is wrong with her and have a real solution!"

My mom followed his instructions and took me to a different emergency department where God blessed me with the best of the best as far as a medical team could be concerned. The ER physician had been working at this particular emergency department since the 80s. He somewhat quickly assessed that I did not need to be going home. He also ordered a CT scan assuming it would be nearly impossible to obtain the scan results from the previous hospital.

I could not drink the solution needed for the scan. The more I drank, the more I would vomit. Everything I put in my mouth returned. This meant I had the disturbing moment of having a tube inserted through my nose to my stomach to drain the contents of my stomach. The physician still did the CT scan, but the dye was inserted intravenously. This great physician began the admitting process and called in the best of the best of general surgeons, who agreed with him that I should not be going home that night. During the early morning hours of May 12th I was admitted to the hospital. Later that morning an emergency colonoscopy was performed.

The colonoscopy confirmed there was a huge tumor in my colon. It was so large that NOTHING could pass through the colon, not even air. They could see a few polyps (which they removed) up to the point that they reached the tumor but they could not get around the tumor to see what was beyond it. This alarmed everyone and they were very concerned that my colon would rupture before they could do anything. Needless to say, I could no longer take anything by mouth except ice chips. This explained to them why I was vomiting so profusely…nothing could get through.

May 13th I had emergency surgery to remove the tumor from my colon. They not only removed the tumor, but 10 inches of my colon and about 19 lymph nodes. The tumor and lymph nodes were sent to pathology to be tested for cancer cells. When I awoke from surgery I had a colostomy. What a shocker this was! However, my surgeon assured me this did not have to be a permanent accessory for me. He stated it could possibly be reversed in as little as eight weeks. In my mind, that was what was going to happen! He stated we just had to wait on the pathology reports, to see if the tumor was malignant or benign before we made those plans.

Let me tell you I was CONFIDENT this tumor was going to be benign. I didn't care how large it was. I had great faith in the Lord and I just knew deep within me it would be benign and I would have my testimony! Approximately May 19th the pathology reports came back. I was shocked to hear the doctor state that the tumor and at least three lymph nodes were malignant. At this point my surgeon wasn't sure what stage of cancer it was, but he knew it was cancer. Malignant…not a word anyone desires to hear, but it was what I heard.

Have you heard these words about yourself or someone you love? Take a moment to write a few notes concerning your emotions as you heard these words.

2 FOR GOD HAS NOT GIVEN US A SPIRIT OF FEAR

2 Timothy 1:7 tells us, "For God has not given us a spirit of fear, but of power and love and a sound mind."

My husband and my mom were with me when I received the diagnosis. The oncologist came to visit and confirmed it was Stage 3 Colon Cancer and that I would meet with her and we would create a plan on where to go from there. She was this cheerful, petite, young woman; and she always spoke life to me when she was present.

When my mom was leaving the hospital, my daughter called her and she gave her the report from the doctors. My daughter then called my husband's phone hysterical. Let's think for a moment…when we hear the big "C" word, the spirit of fear tries to attach to us and STEAL our peace and ultimately KILL us. But remember, Jesus said in John 10:10, "The enemy comes only to STEAL and KILL and DESTROY…" I had my husband hand me the phone and I said to her, "Listen closely to me…this does NOT have to be a death sentence! It can be a new lease on life! It is written, 'All things work to the good of those who love the Lord! ALL THINGS WORK TO THE GOOD OF THOSE WHO LOVE THE LORD, not some things, but ALL THINGS! This IS a new lease on life! I don't know yet what it will look like, but we will get through this journey!"

It was at this time that I remembered hearing Kenneth Copeland share part of his daughter's testimony. His young granddaughter had gotten very ill and her parent's rushed her to the hospital. When the doctors came to them and told them that things did not look good for her and they weren't sure if she would make it through the night, Kenneth's daughter looked at her husband and declared, "NO FEAR! Fear has NO place or authority here!" She stated to her parents that when she made that declaration she saw fear leave the hospital like a dark cloud going out of the window. I said in my spirit, "NO FEAR! Fear has NO place here!"

So, what about my daughter? As I spoke to her and assured her that this was not a death sentence but a new lease on life, an expansion of territory, she began to calm down. I began to instruct each person that wanted to visit me not to bring fear with them. I told them fear had no place in my life or in the room with me. I told them to check their fear at the door because fear would bring death to me.

How has fear tried to attach to you? How has it affected your life? List some ways fear has tried to attach to you, the affects it had on you, and what you did (or can do to kick it out).

3 PREPARE YOUR MINDS FOR ACTION

First Peter 1:13, "Therefore, prepare your minds for action, keep sober in spirit, and fix your hope completely on the grace to be brought to you at the revelation of Jesus Christ."

When you are in school, you don't have a test without preparation, even a pop quiz you have been somewhat prepared for. Do you know that God works much the same way? He prepares us in advance for these tests that we are to endure. I never fully realized this until this journey. We see in First Peter 1:13, "Prepare your minds for action..." The first action I took was to declare that fear had no place or authority around me.

Lying in that hospital bed that night after receiving the diagnosis, my husband had fallen to sleep, and I was just lying there with the TV volume low, waiting on the next nurse or aid to come stick me; and talking to God, and listening for His reply. I remember saying to Him, "Lord, you surely have a sense of humor! You had me teaching through video. You had me teaching a group on being healed of introversion, and even writing a book on it! You had given me a weekly radio broadcast...and now look! I am in the hospital with an incision and a colostomy! I am not asking you, "Why," because I know that is a victim question that will not be answered in this realm, but I want to know, "What is this about? And, what am I to do?"

This is what I heard Him say, "Philippians 4:11-13, 'Not that I speak from want, for I have learned to be content in whatever circumstances I am. I know how to get along with humble means, and I also know how to live in prosperity; in any and every circumstance I have learned the secret of being filled and going hungry both having abundance and suffering need. I can do ALL things through Him (Christ) who strengthens me.'" That's right; He gave me Paul's Words.

So I replied, "What's the secret? Please reveal it to me. I want to know the secret. Show me your glory. Show me how to be absolutely content in any and all circumstances."

Without me even realizing it at the time, God had prepared me months before this journey began. He reminded me of a teaching from Graham Cooke that I had heard many months before, and even shared with others as encouragement. I had the secret all along and He was just about to reveal it to me through this memory!

Graham Cooke said, "We all face circumstances in life that knocks the wind out of us. Usually when these circumstances come for a visit we pick up the phone in a panic and call our friends or prayer partners and say, 'What am I going to do? I don't have the money for these car repairs!' Or, 'The doctor called and wants to see me! What if he has bad news? How will I handle it? If everything was alright they would have just given me the results over the phone! Please pray!' Can you relate to this? But what if we took a different approach to these unexpected curve balls life throws at us that hit us hard and take away our breath? What if we called our friends, but instead of fear and frustration screaming through us; what if we spoke to them with excitement?" Excitement? How can we call friends with excitement when we have just been given a report of cancer or financial woes? "What if we called our friends and said, 'Guess what showed up today? Yes, it's that problem that I told you I had been expecting! I knew it was going to be a doozy because Holy Spirit has been bouncing off of the walls all morning!'"

I giggled because Graham is sometimes comical when he brings these great incites, but there it was in my memory. The secret to being content in any situation is thanksgiving. Thank God for those unexpected, frightening, and frustrating events. Even if all you can say is, "Thank You," you say it until you become thanks!

Yes, oh yes, your flesh will fight it! As I sat there in that bed thanking God, thanking Him for revealing the secret to me; but also thanking Him for this diagnosis, my flesh screamed loudly, "You fool! You are NOT thankful for a cancer diagnosis! Your faith was that those reports would come back benign! Stop that! How can you possibly be thankful for this?" The louder my flesh yelled and screamed and pitched a fit, the more I said, "Thank you, Lord! Thank you that ALL things work for the good of those who love the Lord! Thank you, Lord for your great grace which will get me through this. Thank you, Lord, that you are increasing my territory. You are expanding my reach and opening a door to a new group. Thank you that I can now speak to those diagnosed with cancer and say, 'I know what it is like to have a doctor stand at the foot of your bed and hand you a death sentence; but I know someone who will walk this journey with you and restore your health!'" I thanked God even when all I could manage to say was thank you. Remember, James teaches us, "Resist the devil and he will flee from you." I resisted him through thanksgiving and I had peace which surpasses all understanding. And I remembered Paul's words, "I have learned to be content (thankful) in ALL circumstances."

In what ways have you learned to be thankful in all circumstances? Have you found that thanksgiving brings you peace? What circumstances are you thankful for today (even the challenging ones)?

4 I WALK THROUGH THE VALLEY OF THE SHADOW OF DEATH

In Psalm 23:4, 5b David said, *"I walk through the valley of the shadow of death, I fear no evil, for You are with me; my cup overflows."*

David said, "I WALK through the valley of the shadow of death!" He didn't linger. He didn't visit; and he certainly did not take up residency in that valley! He walked without fear because God the Father, God the Son, and God the Holy Spirit were walking with him. We know this because he said, "You are with me; Your Rod and Your Staff, They comfort me." The rod and the staff…Jesus and Holy Spirit.

Next we see David saying, "My cup overflows." He has come out of the valley of the shadow of death and he is overflowing with Joy! He had a revelation, one that we all must decree and declare and experience: "SURELY GOODNESS and MERCY WILL FOLLOW ME ALL THE DAYS of MY LIFE!"

Goodness here is defined in Hebrew as good, good thing, good man/woman, beautiful, best, better, bountiful, cheerful, at ease, favor, glad, graciously, joyful, kindness, loving, merry, most pleasant, precious, prosperity, ready, sweet, wealth, and welfare. Mercy is defined in Hebrew as kindness, beauty, favor, good deeds, kindness, merciful; to be good, be kind; show kindness to oneself.

It is written in 2 Samuel 22:26, "With the merciful thou wilt show thyself merciful, and with the upright man thou wilt show thyself upright.

In what ways are you showing yourself kindness?

_____

_____

_____

_____

_____

_____

_____

_____

_____

_____

5 DECREE A THING AND IT SHALL BE ESTABLISHED

Job 22:28 states, "You will also decree a thing, and it will be established for you; and light will shine on your ways."

This is one of the most important parts of this testimony. After 11 days in the hospital, I was able to return home. Now, how many of you know this is when anxiety attempts to attach to you and steal your peace and joy? I came home and my house had basically been rearranged while I was in the hospital and no one forewarned me! I was shocked and kind of had a hard time appreciating it because before it was rearranged, I knew where everything was. However, after a few minutes and walking slowly through my home looking around, God revealed to me that these were good changes which would be very beneficial to me in the days to come.

One of the changes that bothered me most was that my vision board had been moved and I wasn't happy with where it was because I could not see it as easily; however, it was a necessary move. You see, when you come home with a colostomy, you come home with a lot of supplies and you have to have somewhere to store all of those supplies. The vision board was moved to place shelves in its place so I would have a place to store all of those supplies that I did not want!

The colostomy wasn't my only point of anxiety though. I was facing 12 rounds of chemotherapy, and everyone else's lives were falling back into place. They were going back to work and back to their normal routines…except my husband. God had told him to be right there by my side, so he did not return to work. In fact, he informed me that he had closed his business and was not returning to work until the chemotherapy was complete. I had to get used to him being with me all the time, which wasn't a bad thing. I was thankful that he was being obedient to the Lord. Here was another test, completely trust God! Completely! Trust Him for everything including our finances! Why is it so hard to trust God concerning finances? I learned to do just that through this journey.

Like I said, everyone else goes back to their normal routine. They are still praying for you, but the visits decrease. They have work and families, and they don't know your schedule for doctor's appointments and infusions, so they just aren't there in the same capacity as before. Anxiety tries to attach to you and lie to you and throw you into a pit of self pity. But we have an instruction and two promises given to us right here in Job 22:28, "Decree a thing, and it will be established for you, and light will shine on your ways."

We have been taught to call things that are not as though they are. I started thanking God for healing me, even though I was still going through chemotherapy. I listened to Kenneth and Gloria Copeland every chance I could, because I knew they could reinforce my faith and encourage me to declare God's Word over my life. Healing Scriptures such as the ones found in Isaiah and Peter, "By His stripes you WERE healed." I just changed it to fit me personally, "By His stripes I AM healed!" Deuteronomy 28:2, "All these blessings come upon me and overtake me because I obey the LORD my God." When Moses asked God who to tell had sent him to the Israelites, God replied, "Tell them I AM has sent you." "I AM..." I realized that my "I AM" statements prophesied into my life. So I changed them. I made certain when I said, "I AM," it spoke life and healing into me.

Not only was I declaring God's word over myself, I was praying for others and encouraging them. I was looking for the "good" in all of this. And the good I found. I learned to receive from God through being in the valley of the shadow of death. There wasn't much that I could do except rest, and it was in this rest that I found Him waiting for me, just as when He came down in the cool of the evening to meet with Adam and Eve in the garden before the fall...

In this rest, I learned that it is truly Him that is my source of everything: life, health, finances, emotional soundness, and peace which surpasses all understanding. It is here that I found healing. I took my last chemotherapy treatment on Monday, November 21, 2016...the Monday before Thanksgiving. I received results from my PET Scan and CT scan on Wednesday, December 21, 2016 which revealed that I AM CANCER FREE! I still have to have scans and tests for the next five years, and each result must say, "cancer free" before the medical field will declare, "You are healed." But I AM declaring today, I have been healed of CANCER by our mighty and gracious God! March 20, 2017 I had another CT scan and once again, the results show NO SIGN of CANCER! Praise the Lord! Thank you, Father!

When I began talking to you tonight, I told you that tonight begins Passover. On the Jewish calendar, God's calendar, the evening begins the day. We see that in Genesis 1, the creation week, "...the evening and the morning were the first day." What is Passover and does it still have significance to us?

6 PASSOVER

Passover is one (the first one) of three main Jewish festivals (Shavuot [Pentecost] and Succoth [Tabernacles, or the Feast of Booths] being the other two), which begins on the 14th day of Nisan (March/April of our calendar) to commemorate protection from the plague of death against the firstborn in Egypt, and liberation from Egyptian slavery.

During the plague of the death of the firstborn in Egypt, Jewish families were told by Moses to slaughter a lamb and put some of the blood on their doorposts and the upper part of the door frame, because the angel of death would pass over their homes when he saw the blood and not harm them. God commanded Israel to keep a Feast of Passover as a commemoration of Him freeing them from Egyptian bondage. He said this Feast was to be kept forever. In the New Testament, Passover refers to Christ as the Lamb slain once and for all.

There are at least seven blessings associated with Passover. In Exodus 23, God promises seven specific Passover blessings to those who obey Him, celebrate Passover, and come before Him with a special Passover offering. The seven blessings are:

1. He will send an angel before you to guard you.
2. He will be an enemy to your enemies
3. He will bless you with provision
4. He will remove sickness from you
5. There will be no miscarrying or barrenness among you
6. He will fulfill the number of your days, and you will not die early
7. You will become fruitful and take possession of the land.

It is no accident that you are reading this book at this time. In fact, it is a divine appointment. You are right here in this moment in obedience to the pull of Holy Spirit to draw you here because God desires to bless you. Just as Exodus 6:6 states, "He will bring you out from under the burdens of the Egyptians (cancer, illness, financial woes, whatever Egypt represents in your life). He is here tonight to rescue you and redeem you with His outstretched arm. He is here to redeem you with His outstretched arm…with His power, His might, His love and mercy, His strength.

If you are reading this right now, it is probably safe to say that your life or the life of one of your loved ones has been touched in some way by cancer or some other illness. Maybe you are overcome with stress because of financial woes. Maybe the spirit of fear or anxiety has tried to attach itself to you. Whatever you need, know this; Jesus took care of it all when He hung on the cross. A curse was given to Adam and his descendants after the fall, but Jesus has reversed the curse with His work on the cross! You no longer have to live under that curse! I believe God has a special gift for you right now. The blood of Jesus has been applied to your doorposts, and the angel of death is passing over. Healing is yours to receive right now. No need is too great or too small for Jesus. The same healing He brought to me is available for you and your loved ones. I would like to pray for you right now.

My gracious heavenly Father,

I come to you this morning lifting up to your throne all of those who have been touched by cancer, whether it has touched their body or if they are the family or friend of the one touched. I ask you to bring them peace which surpasses all understanding. I ask you to touch their body with your healing hands, to assign angels of healing to them. I ask you to remove the tumors, remove the bad cells from their blood. I ask you to cleanse them and make them whole. May each symptom and side effect of chemotherapy and radiation be removed from them. I declare in the Name of Jesus for nausea, hair loss, fatigue, muscle atrophies, neuropathies, weakness, and all other side effects to exit their bodies. They are the children of the living God and joint heirs with His Son, Jesus Christ! I declare that you must go in Jesus name! All cancer, come to attention! In the name of Jesus you MUST leave these bodies! He has given me authority over you through His work on the cross and I declare that you must go in Jesus name! Father, you have given us creation power in our words. I speak long life into each person reading these pages. Your word declares in Isaiah and Peter that "By His stripes they WERE healed!" They were healed past tense, it's already been done! I declare and decree that You are redeeming them with Your mighty outstretched arm!

I thank you, Lord, for my own walk through the valley of the shadow of death. I thank you that you allowed me to see that Psalm 23 is truly about LIFE not DEATH! I thank you that all things work for the good of those who love the Lord. I thank you that I can minister to and pray for each of these individuals. Lord, I consider it a privilege and an honor to bring them before your throne. Father, Your word tells us to "Consider it pure joy whenever we face trials of many kinds, because it is a testing of our faith and produces perseverance," (James 1:2-3). Sometimes these tests feel too hard. They are more than uncomfortable, they are painful and heartbreaking. I thank you, Lord, that You are there with us during these tests and You help us through them.

Father, please anoint each one with Your oil and make their cup to overflow with exceeding and abundant joy. Heal them as a testimony on their lips and for Your glory and honor. In Jesus name, amen.

7 STRETCH

As each year comes to a close I begin to pray about the upcoming year. I ask the LORD to give me a word to focus on during that new year, and to teach me all He can throughout the year on that topic; 2016 was no different. The word I knew I was to focus on for the year was "*Stretch*." I just didn't know what this held in store for me. Those that have heard me teach before have likely heard me say, "I can't teach on something until I experience it..." Well, throughout the first few months of the year we had encountered some slight stretching, but nothing as compared to what would come in May and the months following.

Let's begin by looking at the definition of the word "stretch."

> *Stretch: be made or be capable of being made longer or wider without tearing or breaking. To lengthen by force. To enlarge beyond proper limits. (Harper, 2010)*

"To lengthen by force, to enlarge beyond proper limits..." this is what God was doing to me. Let me be completely honest with you, it didn't feel good. There were so many unknowns. There were so many people I didn't know asking me to trust them with my life! Trust is earned, is it not? How can I trust someone I just met with my life? I mean, seriously, we didn't even have an opportunity to move through the romancing stage of a relationship, to enter into the love which leads to trust; but the reality was they wanted me to trust them. It truly felt more like two meteors colliding, which should bring destruction; but I had to step outside of my comfort zone and attempt to trust them. I had to trust them because I knew that God had given me a divine appointment with the best of the best here, because I had already experienced the worst leading up to this point.

Sometimes we have to experience the "bad" to recognize the good, and both are actually a blessing.

So, here we find the first of January 2016, and the Lord has given me the word "stretch" to focus on. Where do I begin? I look up the definition to see what all I can learn about this word. I also turn to Scripture to see how it is used. I turn to my concordance in the back of my Bible and find it in Exodus 3:20, "So I will **stretch** out My hand and strike Egypt with all My miracles which I shall do in the midst of it; and after that he will let you go." I began to hide this verse in my heart; meditating on it, not knowing how much I would need it in the future. Stretch, in this verse, is Strong's Hebrew Number 7971 and means: shâlach, shaw-lakh'; a primitive root; to send away, for, or out (in a great variety of applications):—any wise, appoint, bring (on the way), cast (away, out), conduct, earnestly, forsake, give (up), grow long, lay, leave, let depart (down, go, loose), push away, put (away, forth, in, out), reach forth, send (away, forth, out), set, shoot (forth, out), sow, spread, stretch forth (out). God will stretch out His hand against the enemy…cancer…and strike it with all His miracles which He will do in the midst of it…while it is happening to you, while you are there…and then it (he, Satan the adversary) will let you go!

Stretch, Strong's Hebrew Number 7971, occurs 995 times in 790 verses in the Hebrew Concordance of the NASB. It is first mentioned in Genesis 3:22, "Then the LORD God said, 'Behold, the man has become like one of Us, knowing good and evil; and now, he might **stretch** out his hand, and take also from the tree of life, and eat, and live forever.'"

It is last mentioned in Malachi 4:5, "Behold, I am going to **send** you Elijah the prophet before the coming of the great and terrible day of the LORD." Notice here that the word used for Hebrew Number 7971 is "send." The LORD is going to "stretch" and "send." Cancer looks like death. It appears as a death sentence and looks like the end. This is a fact. Now let me tell you this…in a sense, cancer is a death, but it doesn't have to be a physical death. You will never be the same person you were pre-cancer. You remember that man or woman that you were and you grieve them; but it doesn't have to be a physical death. YOU CAN LIVE! Yes, your identity has changed; no, it doesn't feel good or even look good, but we know that all things work for the good of those who love the LORD. Your identity is changing, just as God changed Abram's name to Abraham and Sarai's name to Sarah; or Jacob's name to Israel, your identity is changing but I believe you are being promoted not demoted and not killed!

Now let's look at Egypt. Egypt, here, represents this thing that has come against you to take your life! Egypt is Strong's Hebrew Number 4714. It is the dual application of H4693; Egypt = "land of the Copts;" Egyptians = "double straits;" H4693 is the same as H4692 in the sense of LIMIT. "Matsor" is a name for Egypt and it means siege, entrenchment. H4692 is from H 6696: something hemming in; i.e. a mound of besiegers, a siege, distress; besieged, bulwark, defense, fenced, fortress, siege, stronghold, tower. H6696 means to cramp, i.e. confine (in many applications, literally and figuratively, formative or hostile): adversary, assault, beset, besiege, bind up, cast, distress, fashion, fortify, enclose, lay siege, put up in bags. Sounds a lot like cancer, regardless of the type or stage…Egypt for us equals cancer. But remember God said in Exodus 3:20, "So I will **stretch** out My hand and strike Egypt with all My miracles which I shall do in the midst of it; and after that he will let you go." Read this verse out loud, this verse is a promise for YOU! God loves YOU enough to **stretch** out His hand and strike CANCER (Egypt) with all His miracles which He shall do in the midst of it; and after that he (CANCER, EGYPT) will let YOU go!

Now let's see what we can learn about the phrase "My miracles." "My Miracles:" is Strong's Number H6381. It means properly, perhaps to separate, i.e. distinguish (literally or figuratively); by implication, to be (causatively, make) great, difficult, wonderful: - accomplish, (arise…too, be too) hard, hidden, things too high, (Be, do, do a, show) marvelous, miracles, perform, separate, make singular, (be, great, make) wonderful, wondrous. Strong's Number H6381 occurs 102 times in 68 verses in the Hebrew Concordance of the NASB. It is first mentioned in Genesis 18:14, "Is anything too **difficult** for the LORD? At the appointed time I will return to you, at this time next year, and Sarah will have a son."

It is last mentioned in Zechariah 8:6, "Thus says the LORD of hosts, 'If it is **too difficult** in the sight of the remnant of this people in those days, will it also be **too difficult** in My sight?' declares the LORD of hosts."

We get excited about God's miracles. Look at a birth…the mom goes through unbearable pain, pain that seems too difficult, and then she is given this beautiful baby. She would go through the pain all over again to hold the miracle that is her child. The fact is a cancer diagnosis feels too difficult. It brings pain, grief, anxiety; fear attempts to attach to you. You are literally in the fight of your life…a fight for your life. There is nothing "pretty" about it; but is it too difficult for the LORD to heal you? Is it too difficult to believe "at the appointed time I will return to you?" Is it too difficult to believe, "at this time next year, Sarah (insert your name) will have a son (life)"?

I am writing this in the early morning hours of May 6, 2017. Exactly one year ago I was experiencing the worst pain of my life. I had a tumor in the sigmoid colon (pelvic colon) which is part of the large intestine that is closest to the rectum and anus. This tumor was large enough that it completely blocked this part of the colon, which is why I was experiencing the worst abdominal pain I had ever had. I experienced nausea and vomiting because

of the colon being completely blocked; and I was to be my daughter's model in a fashion show to raise money for domestic violence victims. I would not tell anyone except my mother that I was experiencing this pain. I was very bloated…in fact, so bloated I did not know if the formal dress I had purchased would still fit me! I ran to town and purchased a corset to hold everything in place so I could fit into the dress. Now, I was in enough pain wearing sweat pants and a baggy shirt…but to squeeze it all in a corset and formal dress intensified that pain. I was determined that NOTHING was going to make me miss this night. My daughter was in cosmetology school and this was an opportunity for her to show what she had learned with make-up application and hair styles. This was her night to shine and it was for a good cause, and I wasn't going to miss it for a trip to the ER; so I leaned into my own understanding, sucked it up (and in), and pushed myself through the night. I prayed continuously, "Lord, please don't let me pass out from the pain! Please allow me to walk this runway without passing out. Please do not let anyone figure out that I am experiencing pain!" And, He answered that prayer.

This is a picture of her creations for the fashion show. I was extremely bloated and in extreme pain in this picture, but I could not let it show. Thankfully, this was at the end of the show.

Once we got home and my daughter heard me telling my husband how much pain I was in she got very upset. She experienced anger because she felt she had prolonged my pain. She told me I should have gone to the hospital instead of the fashion show…but as mama, I wasn't missing that fashion show for anything in the world! This was her night to shine and I didn't want her worried about me! I really had no idea just how sick I was!

Why am I repeating this account to you now, when I first shared it in the beginning of the book? Because today marks one year, and right now, one year later, I have LIFE! I am cancer free! I am writing this book, I am teaching, I am in school, I am doing ministry work. It felt too difficult for me, especially when I finally did go to the ER and the first ER I went to found the tumor through a CT scan but did nothing except hand me pain pills and laxatives (which increased my vomiting) because the colon was completely blocked. I spoke earlier about my medical team wanting me to trust them with my life…I put trust in the first ER and they let me down. They disappointed me because they were no help and if I had kept going to them I surely would have died. Disappointment can cause you to miss a divine appointment.

Is it too difficult for the LORD? No, it's not too difficult for the LORD. Is it too difficult for you and me? It feels like it, and that is a very real fact. I will not sit here at this computer and try to minimize anything you are experiencing. It is a fact it is HARD! It is difficult.   It is painful. It is frightening. It is discouraging. But I encourage you, do not give up because the truth is, it is NOT too difficult for the LORD! He can and will work right where you are. You are not alone in this for He is surely with you and His rod and His staff (Jesus and Holy Spirit) are right there with you too, to bring you comfort and peace in a very difficult time.

A year ago today, I was being alerted that I needed to go to the hospital. I needed to seek medical attention, help. Something was trying to kill me. Cancer (Egypt: the adversary) was coming to kill and steal and destroy; but JESUS was there to bring me LIFE and LIFE MORE ABUNDANT! "Is anything too difficult for the LORD? At the **appointed time I will return to you, at this time next year, Sarah (insert your name) will have a son (life)**."

Take a moment now to write your thoughts. Acknowledge the emotions you are experiencing. They are real and should not be denied, acknowledge them as a fact; but then write the truth found in God's word. His Word is truth! In Isaiah 55:11 we find it written, "So will My word be which goes forth from My mouth; It will not return to Me empty (void), without accomplishing what I desire (it was sent out to accomplish), and without succeeding in the matter for which I sent it." We also see it written in Isaiah 46:10, "Declaring the end from the beginning, and from ancient times things which have not been done, saying, 'My purpose will be established, and I will accomplish all My good pleasure.' It is His good pleasure to bring you LIFE and LIFE MORE ABUNDANT!

_____
_____
_____
_____
_____
_____
_____
_____
_____

8 GOD PROMISES TO BE OUR PERFECT PEACE

We are often hit hard with storms in life. These storms can overwhelm us greatly. Fear is like a thick shadow of darkness, controlling our every move and decision. Yet reality tells us that so much of what we spend our time worrying about never even happens. Living under the weight of the "what ifs" is a hard place to dwell.

About three months into chemotherapy fear tried once again to attach itself to me. If it could not get me to be paralyzed by the threat of dying from cancer, it would try to make me stop my treatments through the fear of losing my insurance! Remember, my husband wasn't working and I wasn't working so we had no regular income. I was at the half-way mark of chemotherapy and it was brought to my attention that I may lose my insurance before my treatments stopped and before the colostomy could be reversed. This caused me great and terrible anxiety. So, I made up my mind that I was going to stop the treatments right here at the half-way point so I could get the colostomy reversed before I lost my insurance. I made this announcement to my family who, of course, were very upset that I would make this big decision without any discussion with them; and that I wasn't too keen on hearing their opinions. All I knew for certain is I was NOT going to live the rest of my life with the aggravation of a colostomy.

I went for my next appointment with the oncologist. This wasn't an infusion day, just a follow-up. I boldly made my announcement to her. She looked at me with great concern in her eyes and she said, "I know with all in me that you can beat this IF you continue your treatments; however, I do not have the same assurance if you stop it now. I strongly encourage you not to make a life altering decision such as this based on finances." I was shocked! How could I not base this decision on finances? I had none and if I lost the insurance I could see no way to pay for the treatment or the reversal of the colostomy. I did, however, tell her that I would pray about it more and let her know at my next visit what my decision was. She assured me that IF, and this was a big IF, because I had NOT been told I was being dropped by the insurance company, I lost the insurance, there were other avenues we could take to help pay for the treatments; but under NO circumstances did she want me to stop them.

A week later when I went in for my infusion, I learned that the doctor had discussed this with my infusion nurse. I saw anger in her eyes as she talked with me. It wasn't a bad anger, it was a caring anger; an anger that said, "You are FIGHTING for your LIFE, don't you make a decision like this based on FEAR!" She reminded me that I had come too far to back out now. I was doing well with the treatments and I had NOT lost the insurance to just keep on keeping on. She assured me, and re-assured me again, that IF the insurance company attempted to drop me they would help me appeal and everything would be alright. I needed to hear these words from both, Mira, the infusion nurse, and Dr. S., my oncologist. When my family was unable to get into this sometimes thick skull of mine, they were.

I went home from that treatment, feeling a little more peace; but my mind still was not made up. I still did not have peace which surpasses all understanding. So I prayed, "Lord, what is this about? What am I to do?" That very afternoon I received a call from an attorney friend I had been speaking to. She said to me, "Do NOT stop your treatments! I deal with insurance companies every day. Just as your doctor said, the insurance has NOT dropped you. They know they are paying for treatments. If they try to drop you, I will help you appeal it and WE WILL WIN! You stop worrying about this. Focus on being healed. This is distracting you." "This is distracting you..." – She was right! For 3 months I had been focused on being healed. I had been listening to Scripture being read to me in order to keep my faith filled to the brim. I had been encouraging others; and now, I was distracted! Fear was trying to stop me in my tracks! But God! God revealed the plans of the enemy through my family, my medical team, and this attorney friend. So I declared out loud, "I will NOT stop my treatments! Fear you MUST LEAVE! I don't have time for this! My life has a purpose and you WILL NOT steal that from me!" Long story short, my insurance did not drop me. They didn't even try, so you see, it is a truth that so much of what we spend our time worrying about never even happens. I was allowing the enemy to steal my peace! I had to take the authority given to me by Jesus to send that spirit away once again!

God has words of life, of truth, that He wants to speak into your fears. Soaking them in, praying them out loud until they become so familiar they replace the other things in your mind is the first line of defense against fear and worry. There's nothing magical about words and verses, but there is power in them, because they are God's words!

When you feel like you are in the storm, no matter what swirls around us, God promises to be our perfect peace. He assures us that He is constantly with us, strengthening us and supporting us. Let's look at Mark 4:39-40,

"And He got up and rebuked the wind and said to the sea, 'Hush, be still.' And the wind died down and it became perfectly calm. And He said to them, 'Why are you afraid? Do you still have no faith?'"

I was just like these disciples, allowing fear to control my life and steal my peace. The only power fear had over me was the power I had allowed it to have! Let me say that again, and really let it sink in as you read it; the ONLY power fear had over me was the power I HAD ALLOWED IT TO HAVE! God knew that, even if I didn't at the time. Hind sight is 20/20. But God restored my peace through His word, my family, my medical team, and an attorney. I had faith, but I had taken my eyes off of Him and put them on this potential problem that wasn't even there!

In Isaiah 41:10 the Lord tells us, "Do not fear, for I am with you; do not anxiously look about you, for I am your God. I will strengthen you, surely I will help you, surely I will uphold you with My righteous right hand.'" Here in this one verse He gives us two commands and five (5) promises!

COMMANDS:
1. Do not fear.
2. Do not anxiously look about you.

PROMISES:
1. I AM with you.
2. I AM your God.
3. I will strengthen you.
4. I will help you.
5. I will uphold you with My right hand (the hand of mercy).

Write down these promises today and frame them. Hang them somewhere you can see them many times throughout the day as a reminder of these promises He has for you. Everyone of these promises belong to YOU! They are just as relevant today as the day they were spoken through Isaiah! They hold just as much power, and they are absolutely for you!

Jesus said, "These things I have spoken to you, so that in Me you may have PEACE. In the world you have tribulation, but take courage; I have overcome the world," (John13:33). He came to this world so that you might have life and life more abundantly. He spoke to us that in Him we may have peace, and He overcame the world for us! He doesn't say we won't have tribulation, in fact, He tells us that we will, but we do not have to fear those tests because He has mastered them.

While writing in your journal, think of the top five (5) or so things in your life right now that are causing you worry, fear, or anxiety. Give those things over to God now in prayer. Pray that He will help you to keep your eyes and focus on Him, not on the

circumstances surrounding you. Ask Him to help you grow in your trust, believing He is faithful to see us through. Ask Him to relieve your fears and help you remember His truth. Invite Holy Spirit to begin to calm your soul by replacing the fear with the words of Truth you just read. Write down the promises from the passages in Mark, Isaiah, and John. When fear begins to creep in, re-read these promises and thank God for His steadfast love.

My Cup Runneth Over

_____
_____
_____
_____

9 WHEN YOU NEED GOD'S PEACE OVER PANIC

The enemy will lure us towards panic and worry if we focus on all that is wrong. But God offers us confident peace that can never be found in this life without Him.

When I began chemotherapy treatments my medical team went over all of the ins and outs of what to expect during this treatment; what side effects I could expect, when to call them, etc. I was on FOLFOX, also known as FU5. This is multiple chemotherapies combined into one. One of the chemicals in this treatment is Oxaliplatin. This one seemed to have the worst side effects. While taking this treatment I had to be in a controlled environment. If I breathed in cold air, drank or ate anything cold, it would make me feel like I couldn't breathe. Those are the words the medical team used.

The first treatment went off without a hitch. I was tired. I experienced some nausea and mouth sores, but nothing major. I was careful not to eat or drink anything cold, and to be cautious with air conditioning. However, the day of my second treatment, I found out just what they had warned me about. I went into the office and received my infusion. When the infusion was completed and I was preparing to leave, I felt a little funny, but thought it was because I had taken a nap. I exited the office and headed to the elevators to leave. As I approached the elevator, I realized that it felt as if I was having trouble breathing. I spun around, without saying anything to my mother, and headed back to the office doors just a few feet away. My mom was asking me what was wrong and I just kept walking. Once I entered the doors, I looked at the receptionist and said while gasping, "I can't breathe!" Not only could I not breathe, I couldn't walk any further because I felt short of breath. They immediately grabbed a wheelchair and whisked me back into the infusion center and grabbed my nurse. Panic surged through me each time I tried to take a breath, and my muscles were cramping, drawing my fingers in as if I had had a stroke. I turned pale as cotton. My heart rate increased as did my blood pressure. However, when they put the pulse oximeter on my finger, my oxygen level was 99! My nurse kept assuring me that I was breathing because my oxygen level was so high. I looked at her through tear stained eyes and slowly said, "I … feel…like…I…can't…breathe! No…air…is…coming…in!"

She went and made me a nice warm cup of hot chocolate and encouraged me to sip on it. She sent the nurse's aide to get my doctor. My doctor was in with a patient, so the aide got the nurse practitioner to come see me. They wheeled to a private room and performed an EKG just as a precaution because my heart rate and blood pressure were so high and I was so pale. It was normal. As I sipped the hot chocolate, and my throat warmed up, I slowly began to feel like I could once again breathe. My body and mind were stressed over this experience. Even though I now felt I could breathe, my body felt weak and was trembling; but I was better. It was quite the scare, and frightened my mom horribly as well.

Yes, I was actually breathing through this experience; however, the cold air of the office's air conditioning, kind of made my throat feel paralyzed so I could not tell I was breathing. In my mind, I was suffocating; and the panic which set in only made the experience worse. Now, I am thankful that this was the only time in six months of treatment that I experienced this. And also thankful that if I had to experience it, I was still in their office and could receive immediate medical attention. Had this happened at home, no one would have known what to do, although, the medical team had told us to get something warm in me. When you are in panic mode, you can't think or remember instructions. In this instance, the enemy didn't lure me towards panic and worry…he threw me head first into it! However, it taught me what symptoms to look for and how to reverse it before it reached that point again. I learned some valuable lessons through this experience, as did my mom.

In Philippians 4:6-9 we find, "Be anxious for nothing, but in everything by prayer and supplication with thanksgiving let your requests be made known to God. And the peace of God, which surpasses all comprehension, will guard your hearts and your minds in Christ Jesus. Finally, brethren, whatever is true, whatever is honorable, whatever is right, whatever is pure, whatever is lovely, whatever is of good repute, if there is any excellence and if anything worthy of praise, dwell on these things. The things you have learned and received and heard and seen in me practice these things, and the God of peace will be with you." I now had this memory of this experience chiseled into me. I could have focused on feeling as if I couldn't breathe, feeling the suffocation; but instead, I chose to think about the rapid response of the medical team. The great care I received. The lessons learned from this, and how quickly God turned it all around. My mom was right there with me, praying for me all the way through it. Demanding that something be done. As horrible as this experience was, I had a lot to be thankful for. I decided I was not going to walk in fear of this side effect but I was going to follow Paul's instructions and think on God and His Word, and His promises to me in His Word; and He kept me in peace.

The Prophet Isaiah tells us in Isaiah 26:3-4, "The steadfast of mind You will keep in perfect peace, because he trusts in You. Trust in the LORD forever, for in God the LORD, we have an everlasting Rock." Steadfast means resolutely or dutifully firm and unwavering. So Isaiah is telling us that God will keep in perfect peace the unwavering mind because he (it) trusts in Him. As humans we sometimes find it hard to trust God. This is sad but true, especially when someone has handed you a death sentence; but that is exactly the time we need to trust Him most. One of the reasons, I believe, that we find it so hard to trust Him in these times, is because we have no control over them. Our mind finally understands that it has no control over what happens next and the flesh desires to be in control. When I find myself in turmoil over things I cannot control, I simply pray, "Father, I release my desire to be in control of this situation to you." I may have to pray it multiple times because my flesh will fight me on it, but that is exactly what I do. I make a conscious decision that I am surrendering the desire to control the situation to Him, an unwavering mind, and He sends peace.

"For in God the LORD, we have an everlasting Rock…" Rock here means a refuge; mighty God; strength. It is first mentioned in Exodus 17:6, "Behold, I will stand before you there on the rock at Horeb; and you shall strike the rock, and water will come out of it, that the people may drink.' And Moses did so in the sight of the elders of Israel." We can see here that the rock is an image of Jesus. He was struck and bruised for our iniquities so that we might have life; and "by His stripes you WERE healed!"

It is last mentioned in Habakkuk 1:12, "Are You not from everlasting, O LORD, my God, My Holy One? We will not die. You, O LORD, have appointed them to judge; and You, O Rock, have established them to correct." – Jesus is the Rock of our salvation. Holy Spirit brings conviction. God sends ones to judge and establishes them to correct us leading us back to Him, our source of refuge and strength.

"Peace I leave with you; My peace I give to you; not as the world gives do I give to you. Do not let your heart be troubled, nor let it be fearful…" (John 14:27) Jesus promises you peace. He came that you might have life and life more abundantly. Yes, the enemy tries hard to steal your peace and your joy, but you don't have to give it to him! Through Jesus, you have the authority to put the enemy in his place…the pits of hell and out of your life!

Maybe you have had a similar experience to the one I described above, a side effect to a chemotherapy treatment or to some other medication, and the enemy used this to try to attach fear to you. In the space below write about that experience. Look at it through the window of your memory and see just how God restored your peace. Note how He

reversed all the enemy was attempting to do you. Did you learn any lessons through this?
If so, what were they?

_____

_____

_____

_____

_____

_____

_____

_____

_____

_____

_____

_____

_____

_____

_____

_____

_____

_____

_____

_____

_____

_____

_____

_____

_____

_____

_____

_____

_____

_____

_____

_____

_____

_____

_____

_____

_____

_____

_____
_____
_____
_____

10 WHEN YOU ARE WORRIED ABOUT FINANCES

As I told you in the beginning of this book, my husband felt God leading him to close his business and be with me throughout chemotherapy. He did not immediately tell me this. When I came home from the hospital I kept waiting on him to go back to work, and each day I found him home with me. Finally I just asked him, "How much time are you taking off?" This is when he dropped the bombshell on me, "I feel God has told me to be here with you. You have all of these appointments. You cannot do the things you used to do and I need to be here."

I can only imagine what the expression on my face must have been because my mind immediately started racing and filling with questions such, "How will we buy groceries? How will we pay the bills? I might have all of this going on but the electric and water companies will still disconnect services for nonpayment!" I was trying very hard not to let these words come out of my mouth because I would never ask my husband to be disobedient to God; but in my wildest imagination I could not see how these things would be done with neither of us working. And then another thought entered my mind, "What would people think of my husband?" I took a deep breath and slowly said, "OK, if this is what God has told you to do He will work it out." And once again my flesh was screaming! It had the realization that it had lost all control. At this point it had no choice except to trust God…and flesh just does not like to do this.

I had to enter my war room and get before God. He and I had to get some things straight! I wasn't going to tell Him what to do; but I was going to ask Him just what He was doing! And that is just what I did! "Lord! What are you doing to me? Every time I turn around the wind is being knocked out of me! Help me!" And I heard, "Do you trust Me?" And I said, "Yes, but…." And He said, "Do you trust Me?" And I replied, "Yes, Lord, I trust You." I just kept saying that over and over and over and over again, "Yes, Lord, I trust You! Yes, Lord, I trust You! Yes, Lord, I trust You! Yes, Lord, I trust You! Yes, Lord, I trust You!"

I felt my spirit being directed to Psalms, so I prayed again and asked Him to guide me to the chapter and verse I was to read. He began with Psalm 4:3-4, 8, "But know that the LORD has set apart the godly man for Himself; the LORD hears when I call to Him. Tremble, and do not sin; meditate in your heart upon your bed, and be still. In peace I will both lie down and sleep, for You alone, O LORD, make me to dwell in safety."

There is comfort in Psalms. I made it a practice to listen to Psalms each night. I have a Holy Bible app on my phone which will read Scripture to me. I would plug my phone into the charger and pull up Psalms and hit play. I would lie there and listen until I drifted to sleep. I found that in doing this, I rested peacefully and learned a lot. I once heard a Rabbi state that what we see remains external of us but what we hear enters us. We cannot see when we are asleep because our eyes are closed, but we can hear. Faith comes by hearing and hearing the word of the Lord! This nightly practice kept my faith built up strong.

And God did exactly what He said He would do. The entire time I was getting chemotherapy my husband was out of work but not one time did our power get turned off or our water. We never lapsed in car insurance and we had plenty to eat. We put our trust in God and He supplied all of our needs.

Often it is hard to trust God when money problems, debt, and loss mount up high. After all, society tells us that God helps those who help themselves (but this is not Scriptural). God knows what concerns us. He understands our every need, and He is more than able to provide all that we lack. Jesus tells us in Matthew 6:25-34, "For this reason I say to you, do not be worried about your life, as to what you will eat or what you will drink; nor for your body, as to what you will put on. Is not life more than food, and the body more than clothing? Look at the birds of the air, they do not sow, nor reap nor gather into barns, and yet your heavenly Father feeds them. Are you not worth much more than they? And who of you by being worried can add a single hour to his life? And why are you worried about clothing? Observe how the lilies of the field grow; they do not toil nor do they spin, yet I say to you that not even Solomon in all his glory clothed himself like one of these. But if God so clothes the grass of the field, which is alive today and tomorrow is thrown into the furnace, will He not much more clothe you? You of little faith! Do not worry then, saying, 'What will we eat?' or 'What will we drink?' or 'What will we wear for clothing?' For the Gentiles eagerly seek all these things; for your heavenly Father knows that you need all these things. But seek first His kingdom and His righteousness, and all these things will be added to you. So do not worry about tomorrow; for tomorrow will take care for itself. Each day has enough trouble of its own."

Oh what wisdom our LORD has! You have been fighting for your life and doing a great job! You are so valuable! You are so worthy! You are so loved! You don't have to worry. I know, it can be hard not to, but you can train your brain to throw off worry! You do that through the word of God!

It is written, "Make sure that your character is free from the love of money, being content with what you have; for He Himself has said, 'I WILL BEVER DESERT YOU, NOR WILL I EVER FORSAKE YOU,' so that we may confidently say, 'THE LORD IS MY HELPER, I WILL NOT BE AFRAID. WHAT WILL MAN DO TO ME?'"(Hebrews 13:5-6).

And we find in Philippians 4:19, "And my God will supply all your needs according to His riches in glory in Christ Jesus."

Pray today that He will give you wisdom in every financial decision, that He would help you be generous in giving, and to trust Him in providing for your family's needs. Write down the verses that you have read in this chapter and meditate upon them. Hide them in your heart as an arsenal in your warfare for when the enemy tries to throw worry on you like a monkey hanging from your back!

_____

_____

_____

11 WHEN YOU'RE ANXIOUS ABOUT THE FUTURE

Receiving a cancer diagnosis of any kind is enough to make anyone anxious about the future. It makes the future feel uncertain. Things seem to change, you are no longer the person you once were. One of the first statuses I made after receiving my diagnosis went along the lines of, "Trying to learn who this new woman is looking back at me from the mirror. Life as I knew it had permanently changed. I would never be the same woman I once was. So, just who was this new woman staring back at me? What would life be like now? There were many uncertainties, and the possibility of life was one of them. The pressure and stress of it all begins to weigh down heavy on our hearts and minds; but Jesus brings us sweet peace.

Just as we learned in the last chapter, Jesus reminds us not to worry about tomorrow. It is written in Matthew 6:34, "So do not worry about tomorrow; for tomorrow will care for itself. Each day has enough trouble of its own." We do not have to worry, we can find sweet rest and peace which surpasses all understanding in Jesus. Yes, it is a fact that someone handed you a very hard diagnosis, but the truth is that Jesus came that YOU may have LIFE and LIFE MORE ABUNDANT! He loves you and will walk with you each step of this journey.

The Psalmist writes in Psalm 56:3, "When I am afraid, I will put my trust in You." Putting our trust in the LORD is a conscious choice we make. We may even think we have it mastered, and then, "WHAM!" a thought of doubt creeps in and we find we are battling again. We are given Scripture just like this verse to remind us and guide us back to trusting the LORD with all of our insecurities. We may feel vulnerable and naked, but that is when God can do His best work! We find that perfect peace in our total surrender to Him. Our victories come as we surrender and rest in Him. Take a few deep breaths. Close your eyes, and imagine melting into your heavenly Father's loving arms. You place your head on His strong shoulders as He hugs you tightly while whispering to you, "I love you. I know this feels hard, but I've got this. You just rest here." Can you feel His love? Just sit there and rest for a while as He embraces you.

In Luke 12:22-26 we once again find Jesus encouraging us not to worry about our need. He says, "For this reason I say to you, do not worry about your life, as to what you will eat; nor for your body, as to what you will put on. For life is more than food, and the body more than clothing. Consider the ravens, for they neither sow nor reap; they have no storeroom nor barn, and yet God feeds them; how much more valuable you are than the birds! And which of you by worrying can add a single hour to his life's span? If then you cannot do even a very little thing, why do you worry about other matters?" You are created in His image, in His likeness, and your life reflects Him! You are so valuable, so much more than you even realize! Take a moment and meditate on these verses. Allow Him to show you your value and worth.

Today, ask Jesus to help you let go of trying to figure out everything on your own and to trust Him in today; knowing that He is with you always, and will lead you every step of tomorrow. Just rest in Him and in His love. He created the Sabbath just for us, just for this reason, and believe it or not, we can experience this Sabbath rest and the peace which comes with it every day! Meditate on these passages of Scripture and notate what He speaks to you in the lines below. (Psalm 56:3; Matthew 6:34; and Luke 12:22-26)

_____

_____

_____

_____

_____

_____

_____

_____

_____

_____

_____

_____

_____

_____

_____

_____

_____

12 WHEN YOU ARE AFRAID FOR THOSE YOU LOVE

It is written in Psalm 34:7, "The angel of the LORD encamps around those who fear Him, and rescues them."

One of the first thoughts that went through my mind when the doctor gave me the diagnosis of stage 3 colon cancer was, "What about my family? How will my husband manage without me? My daughters are you adults, but they still need their mother. They haven't married yet, they don't have any babies yet. They will need their mother's help with these things. I want to meet my grandchildren! I want to witness their father giving their hands in marriage! I am not afraid to die, but I am not ready! I am 44 years old and my family needs me! What will happen to them? Can they handle this?"

The enemy knows that often he cannot entrap us through what happens to us personally. Our faith is strong enough to handle the attacks he throws at us; but when he starts to threaten our family and loved ones that is a whole new ballgame! He is cunning and knows that he can distract us by attacking our families. Where we will not succumb to fear for ourselves, he looks for a loophole through our family.

Chemotherapy is very exhausting. It consumes all of our strength to fight to live, and the enemy knows that you are weak; this is when he will try to get to you through your family. I remember after several treatments, the poison of chemo had begun to accumulate in my body, making me even more tired. To my oldest daughter it looked as though I had given up. I would move from the bed to the couch and that was about as far as I could make it. Sometimes I didn't even make it back to the bed, I would just rest on the couch for days on end only getting up to go to the bathroom. She couldn't understand why I was so immobile and began to lash out. "You are giving up! I will not sit here and watch you give up! Get up! Move! Do something! Live!" I tried to explain to her that I just didn't have the strength but she couldn't understand. I let her say whatever she needed to say (even when it was hurtful) because she needed to get it out, and I prayed and prayed and prayed! This was too hard for her to watch, and I couldn't even imagine just how hard it was for her.

My husband and I talked and he said to me, "You have to understand, we don't know what to do when the backbone, the glue of our family who holds us all together, is down and unable to live as she once did. You are our glue and our strength. When you are down we feel weak and confused. We, too, are grieving the woman you once were and are having to learn who this new woman is. We love you but we do not know how to deal with this either. I didn't want to tell you this because I didn't want to hurt you. I wanted to protect you from our fear, and we do not know how to battle fear the way that you do." "We don't know how to battle fear the way that you do…" those words hit hard! Hadn't I taught them? In all of these years of teaching Scripture that I had done, had I failed to teach my family how to battle these things while I was teaching the world? NO! I had not failed to teach them. They knew so much more than they thought they did, and just when they needed it, God brought it forth in their memories.

As I prayed over these concerns the LORD led me to Psalm 121: 3-8, "He will not allow your foot to slip; He who keeps you will not slumber. Behold, He who keeps Israel will neither slumber nor sleep. The LORD is your keeper; the LORD is your shade on your right hand. The sun will not smite you by day, nor the moon by night. The LORD will protect you from all evil; He will keep your soul. The LORD will guard your going out and your coming in from this time forth and forever." I shared these verses with my family and I told them, "These promises are not just for Bible times, they are for NOW! They are for me, yes; but they are also for YOU! We are not in this alone. I may not be able to the things I used to do right now, but this is not the end! I have not given up. The lesson that we must learn right now is how to receive from Him! This may not look the way we expect it to look. You see me just lying here on the couch not doing my normal routine, and sleeping a lot; but I am receiving from God. He is sustaining me and strengthening me. He is carrying me when I am unable to walk. He has been teaching me for years to receive from Him and others because there was a time that I could not even receive a compliment. Now, He has accelerated my learning. Sometimes we have to be flat on our backs to learn the lessons He desires for us to learn. Things do not always look as they are. We must trust His infinite Wisdom here, even if we do not fully understand it. He has placed me back on the potter's wheel and He is mending and expanding. We will get through this and we will do it together. I ask you to be patient with me while I am in this learning phase." And I reminded them, "It is written, 'Faith comes by hearing and hearing the word of the LORD.' When you feel doubt or fear, or you do not trust what you see, listen to the word of the LORD! Pray for His understanding to accompany His great wisdom."

He then guided us to Psalm 91:11, "For He will give His angels charge concerning you, to guard you in all your ways." These are promises for you too! They weren't written just the ones living during the penning of these words. They weren't just written for me and my family; they were written for YOU for such a time as now!

One of the biggest fears many battle is that something will happen to their loved ones and this fear seems exacerbated when you have been diagnosed with cancer. Yet the reality is, we cannot always be with them, nor can we always protect them from all that may come their way. But God is with them always, and He is mighty!

Pray that His protection would surround those you love, that His angels would guard their coming and going; and that He would keep them safe from harm. Thank Him that we can release those we love into His care, knowing that He watches over His children, and covers them in His care.

Acknowledge the fear that has tried to attach to you concerning your family during this difficult season of your life. Write them down in the space below. Next, meditate on Psalm 34:7; 121:3-8; and 91:11. What words of wisdom is the LORD speaking to you through these verses? What assurances has He given you? Write these down now, and speak them out loud! Declare His word over your life and the lives of your loved ones, giving it an assignment that will not return to Him without first accomplishing what it was sent out to do.

_____

_____

_____

_____

_____

_____

_____

_____

_____

_____

_____

_____

_____

_____

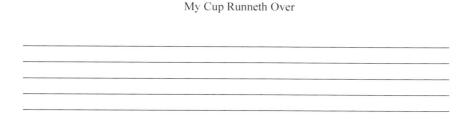

13 WHEN YOU FEEL OVERWHELMED

Once I began to get used to the chemo schedule and everyone returning to their normal routines, and my husband being home with me, I began to feel as if my feet were being firmly planted under me again. I was going to be able to do this. I really could walk this journey and come out on the other side with peace and joy. Then one morning I woke up in a rage! I locked myself in my bedroom and told everyone to just leave me there to please not try to talk to me because I was afraid I would be mean to them and I had no reason to be. I told them that I could not explain it, but at that moment I could not even stand myself and I was afraid I would lash out at them and they didn't deserve that. They could not understand what was going on and they were very concerned. After several hours of being locked in my room, my husband sent for my mother.

My mom got there and I just burst into tears. These were really the first tears I had shed since this journey began. I just sobbed. I could not control it nor stop it. My mom finally said, "Regina, call your oncologist. She can give you something to help with this anxiety and overwhelm that you are experiencing. You do not have to be strong for everyone else. It is OK to let it out, but you also do not have to carry this weight around your neck like a noose. Allow them to call you something in."

The last thing I wanted was another chemical entering my body, but I knew she was right. I needed something to help me cope. It had become too much and I was taking it out on the ones who were being so good to me. I called the oncologist and she did call me in something. It was horrible. I didn't have to worry about anxiety because I slept 95% of the time! I could not stay awake with that medication, so, it was ineffective because I would not take it. When I went back for my follow up with her I let her know how it made me sleep and that I was already tired from the chemo and I just felt I was sleeping my life away. She graciously changed the medication, and this second one was a much better match for me. No longer was I reacting like a rabid dog towards my loved ones, and I could stand being in my own skin.

When the oncologist had discussed chemotherapy, she didn't mention that the buildup of these chemicals in your body would lead to what they called "chemotherapy induced anxiety." If she did mention it, I missed it. I did not recall hearing that side effect.. I can honestly say it felt like it was just too much for me to handle. I felt I could handle a cancer diagnosis, probably even chemotherapy, but the colostomy that was another story. I had extreme stress from the colostomy. I hated dealing with the insurance company in attempts to get supplies. I hated having to use reusable bags. I hated the leaks that would sometimes occur. I hated everything about having colostomy and I didn't have a hope of getting rid of it until after chemotherapy; but with God's help I could get through this with joy.

It is written in Isaiah 35:4, "Say to those with anxious heart, 'take courage, fear not. Behold, your God will come with vengeance; the recompense of God will come, but He will save you." This, my friend, is a TRUTH and a PROMISE for you! He will save you! He has placed you with a medical team who has years of training and who continue their education. He rains His wisdom upon them. Know this, it is OK to take medications to help you with anxiety! You are going through a LOT right now. There is no shame in anxiety medication. Remember, He provides wisdom to your medical team and you. It's OK not to feel strong all the time. You are in a very vulnerable state right now, but that is where you will experience God's presence when you most need it! He has not left you nor forsaken you! He is carrying you through this!

"For God is not a God of confusion but of peace..." (1 Corinthians 14:33). He will restore your peace. He will give you peace which surpasses all understanding. It may not feel like it right now, but you can walk this journey with peace! He loves you and desires to bring His peace to you!

When troubles overwhelm and worry sets in, it can feel like we can hardly breathe. It might seem as if we are drowning in the pressures and fears that life has thrown our way. God can cut through all of that! He is powerful to work a miracle on our behalf. The same God who split the sea and healed the sick is the God who hears your prayers today.

Psalm 61:2-5, "From the end of the earth I call to You when my heart is faint; Lead me to the rock that is higher than I. For You have been a refuge for me, a tower of strength against the enemy. Let me dwell in Your tent forever; Let me take refuge in the shelter of Your wings. Selah. For You have heard my vows, O God; You have given me the inheritance of those who fear Your name."

Take a moment now and tell God what is troubling your heart and soul. He cares.

He desires to help you. He loves you so much He created you in His image. Meditate upon these verses as you sit in His presence and allow Him to bring you the peace which surpasses all understanding.

.

---

14 FACING DEFEAT AND DISCOURAGEMENT

There may be times in this journey that you begin to feel defeated and discouraged, but do not lose hope! Things may seem impossible and harder than you could ever have imagined, but God is for you! He has good plans for you and He is not finished with you yet!

We find it written in Joshua 1:9, "Have I not commanded you? Be strong and courageous! Do not tremble or be dismayed, for the LORD your God is with you wherever you go." – The LORD your God is with you wherever you go, even through a journey with cancer. It began to feel as if every time I had lab work done it would come back with my potassium low. This led to me having to take potassium. The pills were huge and I could not swallow them, so I had to get the liquid potassium. This was like taking an Orange Crush soda and filling it with a box of salt and then having to drink it. It tasted horrible, but it was necessary.

So many of you face much harder struggles than I can imagine. Yes, my diagnosis was devastating; but it wasn't nearly as bad as some others have to face. So many of you encouraged me sitting in that infusion room. It wasn't that we had long conversations; it was your will to survive, to fight against all of the odds. It was your love for yourself, your family, and others. Without even realizing it, you were encouraging me to keep fighting the good fight.

The Psalmist encourages us in Psalm 43:5, "Why are you in despair, O my soul? And why are you disturbed within me? Hope in God, for I shall again praise Him, the help of my countenance and my God." – Praise Him right now, right where you are in this journey. Even if everything in you fights you in this, praise Him! Praise is one of our many weapons of warfare. Praise is also where He can strengthen you when you feel your weakest. "The God of peace will soon crush Satan under your feet. The grace of our Lord Jesus be with you," (Romans 16:20).

The voices in this world, the enemy's lies, and even our own negative words can do a pretty good job of making us feel anxious and defeated. Choose to tune out all that mess, and instead choose to listen to what God says about you. He reminds you that you are more than a conqueror. He tells you not to fear. Meditate on these verses today. Pray that He will help you to have wisdom in whose voice you listen to and that your thoughts would be focused on Him.

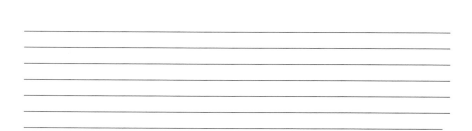

15 WHEN YOU FEEL DESPERATE

One thing I learned walking through this valley of the shadow of death is that there absolutely were days when I felt desperate. Anxiety was trying to grab hold of me, chemotherapy was tearing me down, and I could not do the things I had previously done. Pre-cancer I was in God's word 10+ hours a day digging and studying and teaching. Now, because of the side effects of chemotherapy I could not continue to do that. It left me not only feeling desperate but as if I did not know myself at all anymore.

About half way through my treatments a concern arose about my insurance. There was a possibility I was going to lose my insurance. If this happened how would I pay for the remaining treatments? How would I get the colostomy reversed? So, in my moment of desperation, I was heavily leaning towards stopping my treatments so that I could have the reversal before I lost the insurance. I was so adamant about it that I had spoken to my oncologist about it. Needless to say, she wasn't happy, nor was my infusion nurse. I remember Dr. S. stating to me, "Do not make these huge life decisions based on finances!" I am sure she saw the shock on my face because I did not know any other way to make these decisions. Her office would be wanting to get paid. I wouldn't be able to afford the medication without insurance. I was desperate! But she was right!

We often make some of our biggest mistakes when we make these decisions based on fear and desperation. Psalm 34:4, 6 tells us, "I sought the LORD, and He answered me, and delivered me from all my fears. This poor man cried, and the LORD heard him and saved him out of all his troubles." The LORD sent me these verses in my time of desperation. I read them and I listened to them; because faith comes by hearing and hearing the word of the LORD. As I meditated upon these Scriptures I cried out, "Lord, I trust You! You are for me, whom shall I fear? I see Your hand at work in my life, and I know that I can trust You."

No matter what is causing you to feel the desperation, you can rest assured that God is fighting for you! He says so in His Word! Exodus 14:14 states, "The LORD will fight for you while you keep silent." While you keep silent…you don't have to say a word. He fights for you! He loves you. You are worthy. You are valuable and you are loved! Not only does He fight for you, He supplies you with armor for your protection. We find this armor in Ephesians 6: 10 – 18.

1. Gird your loins with TRUTH
2. Put on the breastplate of RIGHTEOUSNESS
3. Shod your feet with the PREPARATION of the GOSPEL of PEACE.
4. Take up the shield of FAITH with which you will be able to extinguish all the flaming arrows of the evil one,
5. Take the helmet of SALVATION
6. And the sword of the SPIRIT which is the WORD of GOD.

With all prayer and petition pray at all times in the Spirit, and with this in view, be on the alert with all perseverance and petition for all the saints.

One I felt led to do was to pray for others. Praying for others helped me keep my focus on God and prevented me from being stuck in a pity party. Physically I may not have been able to do a lot to help others, but I could pray. I could keep them lifted before the Lord, and I could encourage them when I spoke to them.

Jude writes to us about keeping ourselves in the love of God; listen to what he says about this: "But you, beloved, building yourselves up on your most holy faith, praying in the Holy Spirit, keep yourselves in the love of God, waiting anxiously for the mercy of our Lord Jesus Christ to eternal life. And have mercy on some who are doubting; save others, snatching them out of the fire; and on some have mercy with fear, hating even the garment polluted by the flesh. Now to Him who is able to keep you from stumbling, and to make you stand in the presence of His glory blameless with great joy, to the only God our Savior, through Jesus Christ our Lord, be glory, majesty, dominion and authority, before all time and now and forever. Amen."

My friends, for the days you can't see a way out of your troubles, when desperation raises its head, and you don't see an end in sight, know this: God is near. He reminds you that he's fighting for you. He tells us to stand strong in His armor and in the power of His word. Read out loud every word of the armor of God. Pray that He would help you to lift your head straight up to Him, believing that He will see you through.

_____

_____

_____

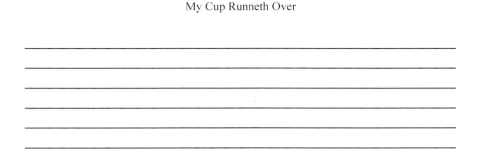

16 WHEN LIFE SEEMS TOO CHAOTIC AND BUSY

"God is our refuge and strength, a very present help in trouble. Therefore we will not fear, though the earth should change. God is in the midst of her, she will not be moved; God will help her when morning dawns. The LORD of hosts is with us. Cease striving and know that I am God; I will be exalted among the nations, I will be exalted in the earth. The LORD of hosts is with us," (Psalm 46:1, 2a, 5, 7a, 10, 11a).

Chemotherapy often made my life feel too chaotic and busy. I had a bi-weekly schedule, but even on the off weeks I had to drive the hour to the oncologist office for labs. This made it feel like I was in the road often. I live in the country, at least an hour away from any major city. It is quiet and peaceful. I feed the birds and the squirrels and watch them eating and playing from my sliding glass doors as I sip my coffee each morning. This is a time of entering into God's presence. As I sit there I invite Him to join me. He and I spend time together talking, listening, and I draw near to Him. He tells us in James 4:8a, 10, "Draw near to God and He will draw near to you. Humble yourselves in the presence of the LORD, and He will exalt you." I know that when I am in His presence all is going to be alright. I can give myself permission to slow down and enjoy Him, nothing else is more important than that.

Even while getting chemotherapy, I would invite Him to the infusion center with me. As the pre-meds caused me to drift into a nap, He was there speaking clearly to my heart during this time of rest. It is written, "God gives grace to the humble. Therefore humble yourselves under the mighty hand of God, that He may exalt you at the proper time, casting all your anxiety on Him, because He cares for you," (1 Peter 5: 5b, 6-7).

Chaos, confusion, and fear are not your garments. He has created priestly garments for you which include strength and power and perfect peace. Again in 1 Peter 5:10 we find it written, "After you have suffered for a little while, the God of all grace, who called you to His eternal glory in Christ, will Himself perfect, confirm, strengthen, and establish you." Paul reminds us in 1 Corinthians 1:9a, "God is faithful…"

Luke recounts the account of Mary and Martha. Mary sat quietly at the Lord's feet taking in, absorbing, all He had to say. Martha, on the other hand, was so busy she could not enjoy His presence. Luke 11:40 tells us, "Martha was distracted with all her preparations…" How often do we get distracted? Thoughts breeze in our minds and we become like a kid in a candy shop, unable to focus on anything, let alone Him. Yet, when Martha says to Him, "Lord, do You not care that my sister has left me to do all the serving alone? Then tell her to help me." He responds, "Martha, Martha, you are worried and bothered about so many things; but only one thing is necessary, for Mary has chosen the good part, which shall not be taken away from her."

How often do we miss the good part because we are distracted by the circumstances of this life? I strive to be a Mary, and sit at His feet. This reminds me of the dream I had in December 2015. I had decided to take a nap one Saturday afternoon. During this nap, I found myself sitting literally in Jesus presence. He was so beautiful and kind. One of the first things I noticed was that my mind was still and quiet. It did not have all of the thoughts rushing through to overwhelm me. My body felt rejuvenated and full of life. It was during this time that I had the true revelation that all peace, all health, all life comes from being in His presence. When we are in His presence, the power that flows from Him brings our bodies into complete agreement with Him and illness cannot remain. One thing I am still trying to learn is how to remain in His presence at all times. I have not yet fully learned this, but I do know that He is always with me in every circumstance.

When days feel full and busy; our time with God may get pushed out. Don't fall for that trap. Time with God will always keep our focus clear and help us move in the right direction. He is able to multiply your efforts and fill you with great peace and joy even in the midst of chaos.

Ask for His help to spend time in His presence, pray that He will help you to say yes to the best, and let the other things go. Spend some time with Him right now. Write down what it feels like to be in His presence. What sticks out to you? Is it the peace you feel? Do you feel strengthened? Do you feel encouraged? Is He speaking to you? What do you hear?

_____

_____

_____

My Cup Runneth Over

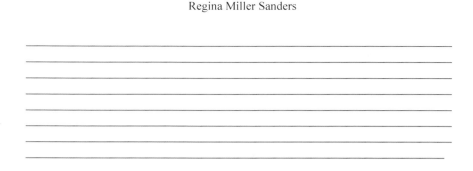

17 REMINDER: GOD IS FIGHTING FOR YOU

I honestly do not understand why bad things happen to good people. All I know is "Why" is not answered in this realm, it's not the question that we need to ask. When bad things come to visit us and we feel we must ask a question let's ask two: "Lord, what is this about? What am I to do?" It is a fact that bad things happen to good people; but the truth is that ALL THINGS WORK FOR THE GOOD OF THOSE WHO LOVE THE LORD! **ALL THINGS!**

Sometimes we need a reminder that God is fighting for us; that He will send a legion of angels to battle just for us! He loves us that much. Yes, He could prevent these things from happening to us, and some think it is cruel that He doesn't; however, when we are facing those circumstances we can be certain that we are not facing them alone! He is right there with us in it all, the good, the bad, and the ugly. Read the words of Joshua out loud with me now: "The LORD your God is He who has been fighting for you. The LORD your God, He will thrust them out from before you and drive them from before you. But you are to cling to the LORD your God, as you have done to this day. One of your men puts to flight a thousand, for the LORD your God is He who fights for you, just as He promised you. You know in all your hearts and in all your souls that not one word of all the good words which the LORD your God spoke concerning you has failed; all have been fulfilled for you, not one of them has failed" (Joshua 23).

A diagnosis of cancer can make you feel all alone, even when you are surrounded by those you love. Your family and friends, and even strangers, try to encourage you but sometimes you aren't sure you want to hear those words of encouragement. In your mind you know that they mean well, but you also know that they cannot even begin to grasp what you are going through, hard as they may try. But there is One who can understand and who will give you the courage, the power, and the might to face this battle and He never leaves you to face it alone. Even when you think you cannot feel His presence, He has not left you. He is not too busy for you. You are worthy of His attention! He reminds us through Deuteronomy 3:22, "Do not fear them, for the LORD your God is the one fighting for you."

Let's see what the writer of Romans tells us in Romans 8, "What then shall we say to these things? If God is for us, who is against us? He who did not spare His own Son, but delivered Him over for us all, how will He not also with Him freely give us all things? Who will bring a charge against God's elect? God is the one who justifies; who is the one who condemns? Christ Jesus is He who died, yes, rather who was raised, who is at the right hand of God, who also intercedes for us. Who will separate us from the love of Christ? Will tribulation, or distress, or persecution, or famine, or nakedness, or peril, or sword? **But in all these things we overwhelmingly conquer through Him who loved us**" (Romans 9:31-35, 37).

David writes in Psalm 118, "The LORD is for me; I will not fear. It is better to take refuge in the LORD. It is better to take refuge in the LORD. You (I think of cancer here) pushed me violently so that I was falling, but the LORD helped me. The LORD is my strength and song, and He has become my salvation. The sound of joyful shouting and salvation is in the tents of the righteous; the right hand of the LORD does valiantly. The right hand of the LORD is exalted; the right hand of the LORD does valiantly. **I will not die, but live, and tell of the works of the LORD!**"

No matter what we face in this life, we are never in the battle alone, even with cancer, especially with cancer. God goes before us. He is with us every step, and He leads the way ahead.

Pray now, that you would stay alert in a dark world, that God will help you to stand strong in Him, and that you would daily sense His presence covering you in all that you are up against.

Where do you need to see God fighting for you today? Do you need Him to provide a strategy for you? In what areas do you need strength (physically, mentally, emotionally)? Where have you seen God fighting for you? What battles have you seen won because of Him? Take a few minutes and write about them here:

_____

_____

_____

_____

_____

_____

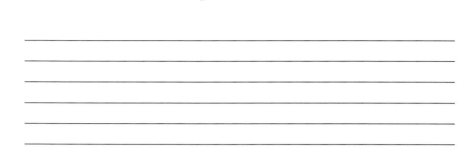

18 YOU ARE NOT ALONE

In the days and months following a cancer diagnosis it can be very easy to feel lonely. You feel as if no one could possibly understand the uncertainty you are experiencing in this moment. Your whole identity is lost. You are no longer the person you were pre-cancer, and in a way, you will never be that person again. It is a time that must be spent getting to know yourself again which can be isolating; and others are waiting for you to be you again. Even now, eight months cancer free, I still remind my daughters, "I am not the same woman I once was. In many areas I have grown, but in some there are still some limitations to things I can do. I will not ever be the woman I was pre-cancer, but this doesn't have to be a bad thing. It just means you have to get to know your mom again." What they don't realize is even though it has been a year since I received the diagnosis, in many ways, I am still having to get to know me.

This reminds me of the account of Sarai and Hagar. Sarai had not had any children and she was old and had pretty much accepted that she would not have children without the help of another. So Sarai went to Abram and said, "Now behold, the LORD has prevented me from bearing children. Please go in to my maid; perhaps I will obtain children through her." And Abram listened to the voice of Sarai. He went in to Hagar, and she conceived. When she realized she had conceived she began to despise Sarai, after all, she was giving Abram what Sarai had not been able to all of these years…a child. Well, Sarai wasn't going to have any of that. Hagar was still the maid and she was not about to let her place herself above her (the wife)! So Sarai said to Abram, "May the wrong done me be upon you. I gave my maid into your arms, but when she saw that she had conceived, I was despised in her sight. May the LORD judge between you and me." So, Abram told Sarai to do with Hagar as she pleased because "your maid is in your power." So Sarai treated her harshly, and she fled from her presence. How often do we flee from God's presence? He won't even be speaking harshly to us, just life throws us these wild curve balls and we step into them allowing ourselves to become injured, instead of pressing into Him and being protected and carried.

When Hagar fled from the presence of Sarai the LORD sent angel to her and he said, "Return to your mistress and submit yourself to her authority." He also let her know that the LORD had given heed to her affliction. And Hagar responded in this way, "Then she called the name of the LORD who spoke to her, 'You are a God who sees'; for she said, 'Have I even remained alive here after seeing Him?'"

I don't know where you are in your journey or what you may be facing, but just as this angel delivered the message to Hagar, I am delivering a message to you. Maybe you are considering stopping your treatments as I once considered, but return to your physicians and submit yourself to their authority. God has given them the wisdom to treat you. The LORD has given heed to your affliction. He is a God who sees!

Let us pray as David in Psalm 25, "Make me know Your ways, O LORD; teach me Your paths. Lead me in Your truth and teach me, for You are the God of my salvation; for You I wait all the day. Remember, O LORD, Your compassion and Your lovingkindnesses, for they have been from of old. All the paths of the LORD are lovingkindness and truth to those who keep His covenant and His testimonies. Who is the man who fears the LORD? He will instruct him in the way he should choose. His soul will abide in prosperity. The secret of the LORD is for those who fear Him, and He will make them know His covenant. Turn to me and be gracious to me, for I am lonely and afflicted. The troubles of my heart are enlarged; bring me out of my distresses. Look upon my affliction and my trouble, and forgive all my sins. Guard my soul and deliver me; do not let me be ashamed, for I take refuge in You. Let integrity and uprightness preserve me, for I wait for You."

When struggles come, fear and loneliness may often follow. The enemy wants nothing more than for you to feel like you are all alone. Be reminded that God sees you right where you are. He won't ever leave you to fend for yourself. Thank Him that He is strongly supporting you right now, that He sees right where you are. Believe His Word – that He cares and you are never alone.

"For the eyes of the LORD move to and fro throughout the earth that He may strongly support those whose heart is completely His," 2 Chronicles 16:9

_____
_____
_____
_____

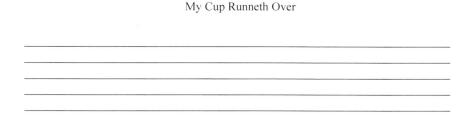

19 BATTLING DEPRESSION AND DARKNESS

Chemotherapy side effects can work hard to get the best of you! One side effect that invades this journey is depression. I remember the first time I experienced this. I had had a few treatments and I had gone to bed fine the night before. When I awoke the next morning I felt it. I was angry, highly agitated, crying for no apparent reason. I desired to isolate myself from my family because I did not want to be mean to them. I felt like just crawling back into the bed and covering up my head, hiding from everyone. I began to question if the smiles I had been giving to others were genuine or if I was just faking it. I have never been one to fake my way through life, so this bothered me even more. My family tried to give me the space I needed, and honestly, that didn't make me happy either. Nothing was going to make me happy!

That statement is more true than I even realized because this was not just depression but depression caused by the chemicals entering my body through chemotherapy coupled with the life changes that come with a cancer diagnosis multiplied by nausea, mouth sores, thinning hair, and all of the other joys associated with chemotherapy. Because this depression was induced by the chemicals of chemotherapy, my usual remedies to master it weren't working…which added to it. I ended up having to call my oncologist to give me something for it which was very hard for me because I do not like taking medications. Let me be the first to let you know that it is completely OK to get medication to help with anxiety and depression. It does not cause God to frown upon you. He, after all, gave someone the wisdom to create it and doctors the wisdom to write prescriptions for it.

Jesus reminds us in Matthew 19:26, "With people this is impossible, but with God all things are possible." The LORD Himself gives us this same reminder in Genesis 18:14, "Is anything too difficult for the LORD?" We find this same reminder in Jeremiah 32:17, 27 "Ah Lord GOD! Behold, You have made the heavens and the earth by Your great power and by Your outstretched arm! Nothing is too difficult for You! Behold, I am the LORD, the God of all flesh; is anything too difficult for Me?"

Depression is feelings of severe despondency and dejection. Now that chemotherapy is over, I still take medication for anxiety and depression because I still experience it. I also turn to Scripture to help me battle it. Verses such as 2 Timothy 1:7, "For God has not given us a spirit of fear, but of power and love and a sound mind." Another verse that brings me encouragement is 1 John 4:4, "You are from God, little children, and have overcome them; because greater is He who is in you than he who is in the world."

This world can feel dark many days. And in troubling times that darkness can hover closely. Yet God is still there. He reminds us that He's greater than anything we face in this life, even cancer. His power is the One who can set us free from the pit we sometimes sink down into. Pray for God's miraculous power to break through the darkness and cover you, lift you up out of the pit, of the place you may find yourself in today. Believe that nothing is impossible with Him. Ask Him for His healing and grace to touch the deepest parts of your life.

My Cup Runneth Over

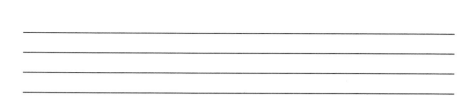

20 FACING FEAR ABOUT A HARD DIAGNOSIS

This chapter is one that probably should have come sooner in this book, but for whatever reason, I feel this is just where God wants it to be. So, I ask you to bear with me with the order of these chapters because God's wisdom is much greater than mine, and His ways are not my ways.

Some of the biggest blows come in the form of a diagnosis...cancer, disease, chronic illness, disability, pain, it can send us spiraling; yet nothing takes God by surprise and He reminds us in the midst of bad news that we still do not have to fear. The Psalmist writes, "The righteous cry, and the LORD hears and delivers them out of all their troubles. The LORD is near to the brokenhearted and saves those who are crushed in spirit. Many are the afflictions of the righteous, but the LORD delivers him out of them all. He keeps all his bones, not one of them is broken," (Psalm 34:17-20). God gives us these reminders, these promises, because He wants us to trust Him.

I think back to laying in that hospital bed looking my surgeon in the eye as he said, "The pathology reports came back. It wasn't the answer we were hoping for. The tumor we removed from your colon was malignant and it had metastasized to at least three of the 19 lymph nodes we removed. This means the cancer moved beyond your colon, outside of the colon, and it will require chemotherapy." I remember feeling numb, not sure I could process this; but also feeling that I had to be strong for my husband and my mom. They were there with me when I received the news. I sometimes wonder how I would have reacted if I had been alone when I received it. Would I have cried? Would I have known what questions to ask? I can only imagine what my reaction would have been because God did not allow me to be alone during this time. I cannot imagine what it was like for you to receive such a diagnosis. I can say that it does feel as if someone is pulling the rug out from under you; but God is there to catch you. He is not going to let you fall. He may allow you to go into the pit like He did Joseph, but He won't let you fall and He won't forget you!

David tell God in Psalm 23:4, "Even though I walk through the valley of the shadow of death, I fear no evil, for You are with me; Your rod and Your staff, they comfort me." David kept walking. He didn't stop. He didn't visit. He didn't linger or build a residence in that valley. He kept moving. He recognized that God provided him comfort... "Your rod (Jesus) and Your staff (Holy Spirit), they comfort me." When I received that diagnosis the first thing I had to do was surrender my desire to be in control of the situation. My prayer was simply but repetitive, "Lord, I surrender my desire to be in control of this situation. I cannot control it. I trust You, whatever the outcome, I trust You. I surrender my desire to be in control of this situation. I surrender my desire to be in control of this situation." The repetitiveness wasn't for the Lord's sake, but for my own. My flesh was fighting this conscious decision my spirit was making and I was bringing it into submission the only way I could think of to do it.

I was very vulnerable and I knew it. I was vulnerable before God and before my family and I did not like it one bit; but I knew that deep down it was alright to be vulnerable. If we cannot be vulnerable with the God who created us, who can we be vulnerable with? That vulnerability made me press in deeper to Him. Sure, I had moments of anger. I was even angry at God at times because I knew that He could have prevented this. I told Him I was angry. Why try to hide it, He created me with these emotions. Sure, some people will tell you that it's not OK to be angry with God or to talk to Him about your emotions; but let me tell you this, He experiences anger too. He understands better than anyone in this world, and He desires your honesty. One thing is for certain, we cannot go above, below, or around our emotions; all we can do is walk through them with integrity. Maintain your integrity with God by being completely honest with Him about the emotions you are experiencing. It's OK to not feel OK! I give you permission right now to admit what you are feeling. He gives you permission to share your burden, unload it, on Him!

I still unload those emotions on Him to this day. I am healed of cancer. All of my scans have come back cancer free; however, the chemotherapy has left me with peripheral neuropathy. I cannot feel my hands and feet, and what I can feel is like I have grabbed an electrical fence and it is sending electrical impulses through my hands with each keystroke of the keyboard. It frustrates me that I cannot do the things the way I could pre-cancer. I have so much to say through these books and bible studies; however, it takes me a whole lot longer to do the things I used to do with ease. It is frustrating, but I am pushing through; even having someone else type for me at times. Why am I telling you this? I am telling you this to let you know that you CAN get through all of this, not on your own, but with the LORD's help! He will not leave you or forsake you!

We can trust Him. Today, pray that God will flood your heart with the assurance that He holds you and will carry you in this life. Thank Him in advance for His healing and strength. Believe His word that assures you He is near to the brokenhearted.

Even if all you can say is "Thank You," say it until you become thanks. I cannot tell you what this feels like, but I can assure it is possible to do! I have done it and you can too! Yes, your flesh will fight you in this thanksgiving, but do it any way!

"He will not fear evil tidings; His heart is steadfast, trusting in the LORD." Psalm *112:7.*

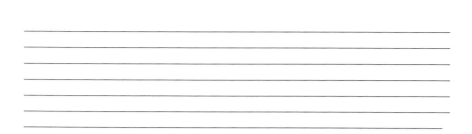

21 FLOODED WITH DOUBT AND FEAR

"My soul, wait in silence for God only, for my HOPE is from HIM," (Psalm 62:5). The mind is a funny thing. Sometimes in the midst of pressures and stress, our minds can start spinning out of control. Thoughts fly into your mind and your imagination attaches to thoughts and begins to build stories around those thoughts. Our mind can create problems that are not there which cause fear and doubt which steal and kill and destroy your peace and joy. We can take each thought captive. We cannot stop the thoughts from entering our minds, but when they try to attach to us we can choose to think about God. When those thoughts try to attach to you, turn to the Word of God, your sword!

Paul instructs us to think about whatever is TRUE, whatever is HONORABLE, whatever is RIGHT, whatever is PURE, whatever is LOVELY, whatever is of GOOD REPUTE (Good report), if there is any EXCELLENCE and if anything WORTHY OF PRAISE, dwell on these things. All of these things that are mentioned here are attributes of God; they are part of His character. When the negative thoughts which bring negative emotions try to attach to you, turn to His word. Jesus said, "I AM the Way, the TRUTH, and the Life..." Do we believe that? What does that mean to you? How do you get someone to trust you? Do you share that trust with them? How does Jesus get you to trust Him? Do our actions towards Him let Him know that He is trusted?

The enemy tries every way he can to afflict us, but God doesn't allow us to be crushed. We are perplexed, but not despairing, persecuted but not despairing...not destroyed. We will go through things in life, but Jesus is right there with us. He is our HOPE when all seems hopeless. Think about this for a moment as it pertains to our relationship with Jesus, relationships are everything. You are responsible for you, your relationships, and everything around you. Resistance is not of love; it is based in fear. Do you fear Jesus? Is a fear of hell pushing you to your relationship with Him, or is your relationship love based? When the relationship is not built around fear we are able to become more intimate, more caring, more like Him.

Going back to our thoughts, you know, the ones that run in and out of your head with your emotions desiring to attach to them and create stories around them...We find ourselves creating problems that don't even exist, doubt and worry can overwhelm us and take control; but we do not have to allow them to have control. We can choose to think about God, His characteristics, and enter into His presence. I have shared this with you before, but in December 2015, while taking a nap, I dreamed I was in the presence of Jesus. He was the most beautiful, handsome, indescribable man I had ever seen. The one thing that stood out to me was the PEACE I felt in His presence. I know why people were drawn to Him like a magnet...I did not have those rushing thoughts drowning me like a rushing river. It was PEACE and JOY unspeakable, indescribable, I desired to remain in His presence and I was not happy when my husband woke me up. I share this dream with you again because I want you to experience that peace. When you finish reading this, close your eyes. Take a deep breath in. Hold it. Slowly exhale. Repeat x4. You are relaxed. Notice where you are. What does it look like? What does it feel like? Is it hot, cold, maybe warm? Now, take a deep breath in. What do you smell? If you can touch it, what does it feel like to your hands? Is it textured or smooth? Now, you see Jesus standing in front of you. What does He look like? What do you feel being there with Him? Do you talk? If so, what do you talk about? What does He show you? Does He hand you anything? What is it? Describe in detail what it is like being in His presence...actually being able to see Him. What does He look like? After you gather these details, write it all down. Date it. Refer to it often. Keep that vision in your mind and it will help you remain in peace and fight the doubt and fear that try to attach to you. Pray today, that God will help you to take every thought captive in obedience to Christ. Pray that you would choose to set your thoughts on Him; that His peace and rest will guard your heart and mind in Christ.

"My soul, wait in silence for God only, for my hope is from Him," (Psalm 62:5).

"Finally, brethren, whatever is true, whatever is honorable, whatever is right, whatever is pure, whatever is lovely, whatever is of good repute, if there is any excellence and if anything is worthy of praise, dwell on these things," (Philippians 4:8).

"For the weapons of our warfare are not of the flesh, but divinely powerful for the destruction of fortresses. We are destroying speculations and every lofty thing raised up against the knowledge of God, and we are taking every thought captive to the obedience of Christ," (2 Corinthians 10:4-5).

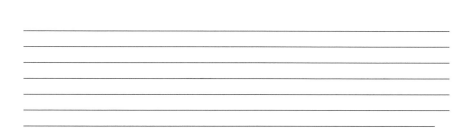

22 DRIFTED OR LOST YOUR WAY

Do you feel distant from God, less intimate with Him than before? Do you feel like there is a great gulf separating you from Him? I understand, we have all been there at some point and time in our relationship with Him; but the good news is that your relationship with Him can be restored.

Let's explore relationships today. Many not only find that their relationship with God is suffering, but their relationships with family and friends are also suffering. So ask yourself, "What's important to you about your personal relationships (including your relationship with God)? How do you see yourself? How would you identify yourself? How do other people see you? Homework assignment: Text, email, call 5 people and ask them, "What is my best quality or my best trait?"

What does any of this have to do with drifting away or being lost? How you see or identify with yourself is how you act. As a man thinks in his heart so is he. What you believe in your mind, you act out and this is what you become. Everything people are looking for change in is their actions or reactions. Your entire life is an action or a reaction. We act the way we believe we should act.

Now for some hard news, if you feel as if you have drifted away or lost your way, you are the one who changed in the relationship, not God. God is never changing. He is always love. He always desires a more intimate relationship with you. I don't tell you this to beat you up or kick you while you are down. I tell you this because it is truth and tell you the GOOD NEWS! The good news is that you can come back into that more intimate relationship with Him! You haven't gone too far. How can I say this? Because it is written is 1 John 1:9. "If we CONFESS our sins, He is FAITHFUL and RIGHTEOUS (just) to FORGIVE us our sins and to CLEANSE us from all unrighteousness." It's not too late to reconnect with Him now. Cry out to Him. Confess that you drifted away, and that you want to return to Him. He will welcome you with open arms because He loves you. You are VALUABLE to Him! You are WORTHY to Him! You are LOVED by Him. No, nothing within us on our own merit makes us valuable or worthy, it is Him in us, His grace and mercy, that give us value and worth!

Psalm 103:12 tells us, "As far as the east is from the west, so far has He removed our transgressions from us." That, my friend, is love.

The east and the west do not touch...they are far removed from one another. When He forgives you of your sin, it is far removed from you so that it is no longer touching you! "The lovingkindness of the LORD is from everlasting to everlasting on those who fear (have reverence for) Him, and His righteousness to children's children, to those who keep His covenant and remember His precepts to do them" (Psalm 103:17-18). He loves you from everlasting to everlasting...forever and ever and ever and ever!

In John 10:10 Jesus tells us the reason, the purpose that the enemy (Satan) comes: "The thief comes ONLY to STEAL and KILL and DESTROY..." He comes for no other reason. His desire is the same today that it was in the Garden of Eden, to take your focus off of God, to lead you down paths that are away from God; to steal your peace and joy leaving you with anxiety and despair, to kill you or your destiny, and to destroy your life, your ministry, or even your family. But Jesus didn't end that message there, He told us why He came..."I came that they may have LIFE, and have it ABUNDANTLY." Maybe your desire for a better life led you down a path that God wasn't taking you down. Maybe you are tired of being sick and tired, broke, busted, and disgusted. This isn't the life you signed up for. We have all been there, now my friend, I tell you as Jesus told us...when we seek Him first, seeking His kingdom and His righteousness, all of these other things will come to us for God is our source. Without Him there is no life, Jesus came that we may have life and have it more abundantly. We have nothing outside of relationship with Him! He is the answer....the Way, the Truth, and the Life!

So, today, I remind you to do the homework above. Comment below how you see yourself. Contact 5 people and ask them what your best quality is. Please share the response in the comments below.

Remember, How you see or identify yourself is how you act. As a man thinks in his heart so he is. What you believe in your mind, you act out and this is what you become. Your entire life is an action or reaction. If you have drifted from your relationship with God, confess that to Him today and ask for His forgiveness. He desires an intimate relationship with you!

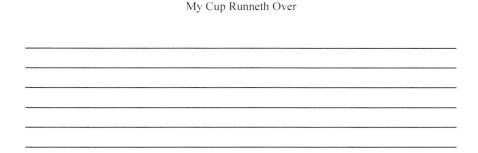

23 NEW STRENGTH IN THE JOURNEY

Even the best warriors get tired, battle-weary. None of us are immune to deep weariness and fatigue, it reminds us of our limitations. But He is forever strong and fills us afresh with His strength and power to stay on the journey.

Paul tells us in Philippians 3:12-14, "Not that I have already obtained it or have already become perfect, but I press on so that I may lay hold of that for which also I was laid hold of by Christ Jesus. Brethren, I do not regard myself as having laid hold of it yet; but one thing I do; forgetting what lies behind and reaching forward to what lies ahead, I press on toward the goal for the prize of the upward call of God in Christ Jesus." Maybe you have been fighting a battle for your health or your children. Your heart is hurting, tired, and weary. But my friend, don't give up. Rest in the Lord. He provided us a day of rest, the Sabbath day. Genesis 2:2-3 tells us, "By the seventh day God completed His work which He had done, and He rested on the seventh day from all His work which He had done. Then God blessed the seventh day and sanctified it, because in it He rested from all His work which God had created and made." God rested, why should we think that we don't need rest. Worry and strife lays heavy on your heart and it works to steal your peace which also robs you of the rest.

We read in Isaiah 40:30-31, "Though youths grow weary and tired, and vigorous young men stumble badly, yet those who wait for the LORD will gain new strength; they will mount up with wings like eagles, they will run and not get tired, they will walk and not become weary."

We grow weary when we carry heavy burdens, but God tells us through Isaiah that those who wait for the LORD will gain new strength. "Yet those who wait:" is Strong's Hebrew number 6960; it means to bind together, i.e. collect; to expect:- gather (together), look, patiently, tarry, wait (for, on, upon). It occurs 53 times in 35 verses in the Hebrew Concordance of the NASB. It is first mentioned in Genesis 1:9, "Then God said, 'Let the waters below the heavens be gathered into one place, and let the dry land appear'; and it was so." It is last mentioned in Micah 5:7, "Then the remnant of Jacob will be among many peoples like dew from the LORD, like showers on vegetation which do not wait for man or delay for the sons of men."

Strength here is Strong's Hebrew number 3581. It means to be firm; vigor, literally (force, in a good or bad sense) or (capacity, means produce) :- ability, able, force, fruit, might, power, or powerful, wealth. It occurs 124 times in 119 verses in the Hebrew Concordance of the NASB. It is first mentioned in Genesis 4:12, "When you cultivate the ground, it will no longer yield its strength (fruits) to you; you will be a vagrant and a wanderer on the earth." It is last mentioned in Zechariah 4:6, "Then he said to me, 'This is the word of the LORD to Zerubbabel saying, 'Not by might nor by power, but by My Spirit,' says the LORD of hosts." By waiting on the LORD we are being gathered to Him, bound to Him. When we are bound to Him we gain His strength, vigor, might, power, and wealth.

Yes, life gets hard and we get weary; but God is forever strong and fills us afresh with His strength and power to stay on the journey. Now, imagine the desired outcome of whatever it is that has you wearied...and know that God is able to do far more abundantly beyond all that we ask or think, according to the power that works within us. He will not only provide the outcome that you desire, He will do it more abundantly than you can even imagine.

.

_____

_____

_____

_____

_____

_____

_____

_____

_____

_____

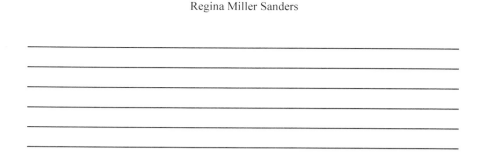

24 WHEN YOU FEEL UNDERVALUED

There are times in life where we just feel undervalued, insignificant, and as if we have no voice. It's not that others make us feel this way, it is our own broken self-image. Feeling unloved and undervalued can lead us to feeling insignificant in this life. It can stir up worry deep within that we have no lasting value or real purpose here, especially when you are fighting cancer, fighting for your very life; and it's just not true!

God declares to you in Jeremiah 29:11, "For I know the plans that I have you,' declares the LORD, 'plans for welfare and not for calamity to give you a future and a hope." - I have heard people say things like, "This verse isn't for you and I...it is specifically for those Jeremiah was speaking to." Let me assure you, THIS VERSE ABSOLUTELY IS RELEVANT TO TODAY! It IS for YOU! God sees you as valuable and worthy; so much so, that He has good plans for you which offer you a future and a hope! Repeat after me, "God has good plans for ME! He loves ME! His plans are for my welfare and not for calamity! He gives ME a FUTURE and a HOPE! This, my friend, is TRUTH!

Next we will explore Isaiah 43:1-4, "But now, thus says the LORD, your Creator, O Jacob, and He who formed you, O Israel, 'Do not fear, for I have redeemed you; I have called you by name; you are Mine! When you pass through the waters, I will be with you; and through the rivers, they will not overflow you. When you walk through the fire, you will not be scorched, nor will the flame burn you.

For I am the LORD your God, The Holy One of Israel, your Savior. I have given Egypt as your ransom, Cush and Seba in your place. Since you are precious in My sight, since you are honored and I love you, I will give other men in your place and other peoples in exchange for your life."

God says here:

1. I have redeemed you.
2. I have called you by name.
3. You are Mine.
4. I will be with you.
5. I am your savior.
6. You are precious in My sight.
7. You are honored.
8. I love you.

Are you starting to see how valuable you are to God? He sees you as valuable, worthy, and loved so much by Him. "The LORD your God is in your midst, a victorious warrior. He will exult over you with joy, He will be quiet in His love, He will rejoice over you with shouts of joy," (Zephaniah 3:17). God is in your midst...He is there with you and He is a victorious warrior on your behalf! He exults over you with joy. He rejoices over you with shouts of joy! God has destined us with specific purposes and callings in this life. He loves us with an everlasting love and fills us with His hope, constantly reminding us that He is leading us.

In Jesus, you are a new creation. Through the Holy Spirit you are able to do all the works that Jesus did, and even greater works. You are a supernatural being because of your new birth in Christ. In your spirit man, you are fully righteous and made in the image and likeness of Christ. His nature and character have been given to you. His power and glory have been given to you. By Christ's amazing promises and grace, you are filled with all that He is and all that He has.

Miracles, signs, and wonders follow you when you preach the good news of the Kingdom, for the Lord Himself confirms the Word you proclaim. In the glorious name of Jesus, you create light in the darkness and order in chaos by calling those things that are not as though they are. In Christ, you have power over all the works of the enemy and nothing harms you. The strongholds of sickness, disease, oppression, possession, and demonic attack are under your feet when you take dominion in Christ. You go forth in the mighty name of Jesus that is more powerful and carries more authority than any other name.

The invisible realm of the Kingdom of God has been granted to you through the eternal, unbreakable covenant that Christ made on your behalf. You heavenly Father has chosen gladly to give you the Kingdom. You have access to the throne room and the heavenly realms by faith through the blood of Christ. You enter with boldness and confidence before the throne of grace and obtain grace and mercy to help in the time of need.

The eyes of your heart and understanding are opened by the Spirit of God, so that you will know the hope of your calling in Christ. The God of your Lord Jesus Christ, the Father of glory, gives you the spirit of wisdom and of revelation in the knowledge of the Godhead and opens your understanding to know the surpassing greatness of Christ's power toward you and to all who believe. These are in accordance with the working of the strength of His might. You are seated with Christ at the right hand of the Father in heavenly places, far above all rule and authority and power and dominion, and every name that is named not only in this age but also in the one to come.

Through Christ, you have come to the city of the living God, the heavenly Jerusalem, and to myriads of angels, to the general assembly and church of the firstborn who are enrolled in heaven and to God, the Judge of all, and to the spirits of the righteous made perfect, and to Jesus, the mediator of a new covenant, and to the sprinkled blood, which speaks better than the blood of Abel. You have received a kingdom that cannot be shaken and therefore you show gratitude by which you may offer to God an acceptable service with reverence and awe. Your God is a consuming fire.

You are an eternal being, and Eternal Life dwells within you. Therefore, you are not limited to the restraints of time and distance. as the Spirit leads, you can perform supernatural acts like Jesus did, such as walking on water, walking through walls, feeding multitudes with miraculous provision, changing substance like water to wine, alerting weather patterns, being lifted up off the earth, raising the dead and working extraordinary miracles.

Angels are dispatched into divine assignments when you declare the Word of God, for they obey the voice of the Lord's Word that you speak! The words of Jesus are spirit and life. Angels ascend and descend upon you because Christ dwells in you. They are ministering spirits sent by God to help you in your mission on the earth. Even when you do not sense them or see them, they are with you to protect you and minister to you. As a supernatural being, your senses are exercised to discern good and evil, and you choose good. You are able to see, hear, and feel the invisible Kingdom realm around you.

You are the temple of Holy Spirit. Your being is filled with glory when you remember and proclaim the goodness of God. The Lord is good and His mercy endures forever. Because Christ dwells in you, you live under the open heaven, and blessings come upon you and overtake you. You are blessed with every spiritual blessing in the heavenly places in Christ. You are a supernatural being encountering Christ and His Kingdom. You bring glory to God through your obedience to Him and by the word of your testimony.

Pray today that you would be aware of His presence, loving you, guiding

you, directing you with purpose and hope. Ask God to help you see
yourself as He sees you, His treasured child, cherished, and greatly valued.

_____

_____

_____

_____

_____

_____

_____

_____

_____

_____

_____

_____

_____

_____

_____

_____

_____

_____

_____

_____

_____

_____

_____

_____

_____

_____

_____

_____

_____

_____

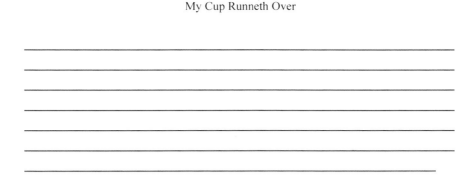

25 FEELING LIKE GOD HAS FORGOTTEN YOU

It is written, "The LORD'S lovingkindnesses indeed never cease, for His compassions never fail. They are new every morning; great is your faithfulness," (Lamentations 3:22-23).

There are times in our lives when we totally feel as if the Lord has forgotten us. We feel that we are walking through this life alone with no guidance and blind! We cry out to God, "Please open this door. Lord, I am waiting! You know I need this..." And it seems He is silent. Is He truly silent, or is He speaking but we don't want to hear what He is telling us? Is He gently nudging us down a different path than the one we think we should be on? Is fear holding you back from taking the first step down the path He is guiding you towards? In John 10:10 Jesus tells us, "The enemy comes only to steal and kill and destroy..." He will send fear to attach to you in order to keep you from walking down the path God has chosen for you. Sometimes it is scary to take that first step because we can't see the whole picture and we don't want to fail. It feels insecure, but the truth is, going down the path that God has chosen for you offers you the most security!

We are reminded in Philippians 1:6, "For I am CONFIDENT of this very thing, that He who began a good work in you WILL PERFECT IT until the day of Christ Jesus."

He started this good work in you! Yes, you may have been praying for three years for this particular thing, and for three years He has been preparing you for your DESTINY! Remember, He has GOOD plans for you which offer you a FUTURE and a HOPE, plans for your WELFARE NOT calamity! He hasn't forgotten you, He is nudging you down the path that He knows you need to be on.

How can I say this with such confidence? For three years He has been guiding me down a particular path in addition to the ministry work that I do. I have picked it up, looked it over, and laid it back down. He let me wander for a while, then He brought me back to it. Again, I picked it up, inquired about it, explored it, and laid it back down. The third time He brought me to it, He gave me a divine appointment with someone. I listened to them, truly listened, with an open mind. I picked it up. I explored it; and I said, "Yes, Lord. This is the path you want me to take and I will go where you send me!"

If I had continued to lean into my own understanding I would have missed this great opportunity the Lord was offering me. In Isaiah 55:8-9 the Lord tells us, "For My thoughts are not your thoughts, nor are your ways My ways' declares the LORD. 'For as the heavens are higher than the earth, so are My ways higher than your ways and My thoughts than your thoughts."

Don't miss the great opportunity He is offering you today because you are listening to fear. Kick that fear to the curb. Remember 2 Timothy 1:7 which states, "For the LORD has not given us a spirit of fear, but of POWER, LOVE, and a SOUND MIND!" Fear is NOT your garment, so don't wear it! Throw it in the trash and take that first step down the directed path from the Lord. You won't be sorry! His opportunity for your destiny is knocking, will you open the door? Will you step across the thresh hold into the destiny He has planned for you? He has not forgotten you, He is leading you towards those great plans He has for you! Come on, let's walk together!

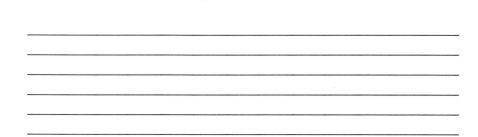

_____

_____

_____

_____

_____

_____

26 WEARY AND BURDENED

Today, many of you are caring heavy burdens. You feel as if you have this weight on your shoulders, Your back is tense and throbbing. Your neck hurts and causes you to have tension headaches. You can release all of that today. You don't have to carry that burden any more. Place it in Jesus' hands, He is offering to carry it for you.

Jesus said, "Come to Me, all who are weary and heavy-laden, and I will give you rest. Take My yoke upon you and LEARN from Me, for I am GENTLE and HUMBLE in heart, and YOU WILL FIND REST FOR YOUR SOULS. For My yoke is easy and My burden is light," (Matthew 11:28-30). He will give you rest today. He will give you peace which surpasses all understanding. Jesus loves you and He doesn't want you to make yourself sick from worry and stress. He will carry your stress and burdens.

It is written, "Cast your burden upon the LORD and He will sustain you; He will never allow the righteous to be shaken," (Psalm 55:22).

Our God is full of power, strength, might; He can handle the loads that we cannot. Today, cast whatever care you have upon Him. He able to provide protection for your children, and to send the right people to them. He is able to heal your body, to heal your family. Cry out to Jesus today. We are not equipped for the types of burdens we try to shoulder on our own. But He is! And He promises to give us strength and rest as we give our burdens to Him.

The prophet Isaiah said, "Do you not know? Have you not heard? The everlasting God, the LORD, the Creator of the ends of the earth does not become weary or tired. His understanding is inscrutable. He gives strength to the weary. And to him who lacks might He increases power."

He doesn't get weary or tired; He will carry all of the load for you. Lay it all down to Him today. Release that heavy load and allow Him to fill you with His peace and joy which give strength and power to you.

I encourage you today to meditate upon these Scriptures and as you do, allow them to fill you to full. Receive His blessing and give Him the heavy load. Pray for His rest and assurance today that He will care for all that concerns you. Ask Him to fill you with His peace.

_____

_____

_____

_____

_____

_____

_____

_____

_____

_____

_____

_____

_____

_____

_____

_____

_____

_____

_____

_____

_____

_____

_____

_____

_____

_____

_____

_____

_____

_____

_____

_____

_____

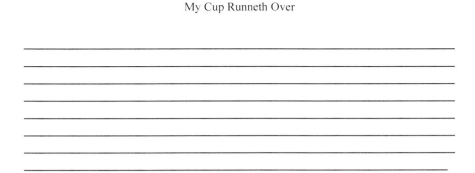

27 TOO BROKEN

There are times when you feel like you just can't go on. The weight of the world has become too heavy. The hurt is too deep and it is sucking the life out of you. You feel shattered into a million pieces, and it even feels like some of those pieces have been kicked under the couch never to be found again making repair impossible. Can you relate to what I am saying? These times of brokenness may forever change our lives but our God is Healer and Restorer of the broken. He is able to make all things new and to give you beauty for your ashes.

The prescription for this brokenness is worship. I know, I know, you may be thinking, "Worship? How can I possibly worship when I feel like this?" Isaiah tells us, "Shout for joy, O heavens! And rejoice, O earth! break forth into joyful shouting, O mountains! For the LORD has comforted His people and will have compassion on His afflicted!" (Isaiah 49:13). The Lord is bringing comfort to you! He has sent forth Holy Spirit to bring you comfort. The 1640s definition of comfort was STRENGTH! So He sent forth Holy Spirit so that you may be "Together with STRENGTH!"

I heard a story of China man who was a potter. Many of the vessels he had created had become worn and cracked showing their age, and leaking. When he repaired the vessels he used gold. This made the vessel more valuable and beautiful. It allowed others to see where leaks had sprung, where wear and tear had taken its toll. The gold was like a road map showing everything the vessel had been through, and it showed the potter's love for it. The potter represents God, and the vessel represents you. Yes, there are times we are broken, and we feel that we are too broken to be repaired but nothing is impossible for God! NOTHING! "And He has said to me, 'My grace is sufficient for you, for power is perfected in weakness.' Most gladly, therefore, I will rather boast about my weaknesses, so that the power of Christ may dwell in me," (2 Corinthian 12:9). You are more valuable to God than precious stones, silver, or gold! He is repairing the cracks with His light and love to place upon your lips a testimony which brings comfort to others as you share, and glory to Him!

The writer of Hebrews exhorts us, "Therefore, let us draw near with confidence to the throne of grace, so that we may receive mercy and find grace to help in time of need"(Hebrews 4:16).

We are able to approach this throne of grace because of Jesus unfailing love for us. The veil was torn, allowing us entrance to the throne of grace (God) because of Jesus work on the cross.

I do not know what has broken you today, but I do know that God loves you. It is His delight to not only restore you but to increase you. Today, pray and trust God, without doubt, to take every broken piece of your life and put it together into a new and beautiful design. Choose to set aside fearful, anxious thoughts, and set your mind on what is true. Jesus said, "I AM the Way, the Truth, and the Life." Thank Him that His grace is sufficient and His power is made perfect in weakness.

28 ONE SURVIVOR TO ANOTHER

I come to you as a survivor! I beat stage 3 colon cancer. No, the battle wasn't easy, yet, it also wasn't as hard as some of the battles some of you are facing. I didn't win this battle alone, but I did it with the help of the LORD, and that is how you will survive!

"They said, 'There must be an inheritance for the survivors of Benjamin, so that a tribe will not be blotted out from Israel,'" (Judges 21:17). You are a survivor and there is an inheritance for you! A survivor is a person remaining alive after an event in which others have died; a person who copes well with difficulties in their life. The Hebrew definition of survivor as found in Judges 21:17 is, "Deliverance, an escaped portion, remnant; to bring into security; cast forth, slip out." God is delivering you from this diagnosis of cancer. The enemy comes only to steal and kill and destroy, but Jesus said that He came that YOU might have LIFE, and LIFE MORE ABUNDANT! He doesn't lie, and He is giving you an inheritance with this deliverance. Inheritance here is a possession, something occupied; a conquest; to occupy, driving out previous tenants and possessing in their place. He is driving out cancer (previous tenants) and He is possessing in their place! You have a purpose and He is not finished with you yet!

I know this battle is hard, but don't you give up! I know you are tired, and I am here to tell you that it is OK to rest. You don't have to be superwoman/man. God has all the super that you need. There is healing in resting in Him. As Dr. S told my husband on a few occasions, "Let her rest now and save her strength for the fun stuff." You do that, let others help you. I know that it can be so hard to receive from others, especially if you have been very independent; however, God sends others to us to bless us and if we refuse their help we may rob them of the blessing He desires to give them. Allow them to be obedient to Him by allowing them to help you. At this time you need the help, and you may still need some once your treatments have ended; but that is OK. Your family and your friends love you and they want to help you; and God sends them to you for such a time as this. You may have to tell them what it is that you need them to do. Don't be bashful, speak up! Do not allow the enemy to put the garments of guilt and shame on you. He will try, but you refuse them! They are not your garments. Your garments are of royalty! Allow your family and friends to treat you as the king or queen that you are!

Part of the healing process is seeing yourself healed and experiencing it first in your imagination. Do you remember the tower of Babel? Let's look for a moment at Genesis 11:6, "The LORD said, 'Behold, they are one people, and they all have the same language. And this is what they began to do, and **now nothing which they purpose (imagine) to do will be impossible for them**." Nothing which they imagine will be impossible for them, and they were being disobedient! How much more power does your imagination hold when it is being influenced by the will of God? Yes, it is God's will to heal you! I fully believe that! It is done! Now, you need to see it and experience it in your imagination and bring it into this reality. What does being healed look like to you? Does it have a smell? Does it have a color? What does it sound like? Is it hot, warm, or cold? Reach out, touch it. Is it smooth or textured? What does it taste like? Look around you, where are you standing? Are you alone? Are there clouds in the sky or is it clear? Is the sun shining brightly? Are there hills, trees, or rivers? What about wildlife? Is any present? – God tells us in Isaiah and 2 Peter, "By His stripes you WERE healed." He used past tense to let us know that it has already been accomplished! He gave us two witnesses! No good gift will He withhold from you because He is your loving Father.

You may be thinking, "But it would take a miracle to heal me!" That's alright! He still performs miracles! Remember, Jesus said even greater works will you do. You will do/see miracles, signs and wonders. They will follow you! He wasn't just talking to His disciples; He is talking to YOU!

"You will also decree a thing, and it will be established for you; and light will shine on your ways," (Job 22:28). Patricia King wrote a book titled, 'Decree a thing, and it shall be established-Job 22:28." In this book she took Scripture and made declarations for us to declare over our lives. God placed this book in my hands the week before I was diagnosed with cancer. He placed it on my heart to begin declaring His word over my life. This is giving His word an assignment. He tells us in Isaiah 55:11 that His word will not return to Him void without first accomplishing what it was sent out to do. Do you believe

Him? If you believe Him, start declaring His word today, giving it an assignment over your life and watch the results come in! I am going to share with you and exert from Patricia's book. May it be as powerful for you as it was and is for me!

"Rejuvenation: Bless the LORD, O my soul, and all that is within me, bless His holy name. Bless the Lord, O my soul, and forget not all His benefits; Who forgives all you (my) iniquities, Who heals all your (my) diseases; Who redeems your (my) life from destruction, Who crowns you (me) with lovingkindness and tender mercies, Who satisfies your (my) mouth with good things, So that your (my) youth is renewed like the eagle. – Psalm 103:1-5

In Jesus' name I decree that my youth is renewed like the eagle as I am renewed in the spirit of my mind. I watch over my heart with all diligence because from it flows the issues of life. What I allow in my mind and heart affects my body and the state of my life. Therefore my body is rejuvenating daily because I am focused on the truth, goodness, and great benefits of the Lord.

I do not allow sin to enter my life, and therefore the consequences of sin (which is the spirit of death that oppresses the body and mind) has no hold on me. If I do sin, I repent and am forgiven and cleansed from all unrighteousness, guilt, condemnation, and shame because of Christ's great mercy. My body is completely free from the destructive power of sin. The law of the spirit of life in Christ Jesus has set me free from the law of sin and death. I do not allow unforgiveness, bitterness, or offense to have place in my life. Therefore, my life and body are free from these destructive contaminants.

Jesus is LIFE and LIGHT. The words He speaks are spirit and life. Therefore I am filled afresh with His ageless, eternal Life and Light when I focus on Him and drink of His promises, declaring their power into my body, soul, and spirit.

In Jesus' name I forth His Spirit, Life, and Light to fill every cell, organ, and fiber of my being. I meditate on His Spirit, Life, and Light filling my mind, emotions, organs in the head, neck, chest, abdomen, back, legs, arms, feet, and hands. Come Spirit, Life, and Light of Christ. Fill me. Renew me. I speak renewal throw the power of Jesus into every organ of my body. I speak to my skin (the largest organ of my body), and command rejuvenation and elasticity to be restored to every cell of it. Skin, receive the glory of God in Jesus' name. I call forth the glory of God to arise, shine, and appear on me as Isaiah prophesied and as was seen on both Jesus and Moses.

I speak to my sight and hearing in the name of Jesus and call forth excellence and precision into these organs of my body. I command health and strength to all my bones, muscles, tendons, and joints. I decree that my heart and circulatory system are vibrant in Christ, functioning at optimum levels of performance. In Christ's name, I speak health and rejuvenation to all the digestive, endocrine, hormonal, immune, reproductive, nerve, electrical, and elimination organs of my body.

I care for my mind and emotions and, as a result, I think only on those things that are true, honorable, right, pure, good, lovely, and all that is of good report. I am anxious for nothing because I submit to the Lord all that concerns me. I reject negative thoughts and emotions and cast all my cares upon Him because He cares for me. As a result, my body, mind, and emotions have no stress – only peace. I am kept in perfect peace because I set my mind and heart on Him. I have the mind of Christ, and my thinking processes are sharp.

My youth is renewed daily in Christ. I abide in Him and His Life flows in and through me. When I am weary, God increases strength in me. When I lack might, He increases power. I run and do not get weary. I walk and do not faint, for the Lord renews my strength when I wait on Him. I mount up with wings like the eagle.

I always yield fruit and will be full of fresh vision all the days of my life. Like Caleb, I will still be pursuing the fulfillment of God-given destiny after 85 years of age, being full of life, energy, and ability.

I soak in His presence and glory. I receive refreshment and impartation into every part of my being. Blessed be the name of the Lord who renews and rejuvenates my body, soul, and spirit daily! As my days are, so shall my strength be. I am fully satisfied in Christ all the days of my life.

Scripture References: Exodus 34:30; Joshua 14:11; Psalm 92:14, 103:1-5; Proverbs 4:23; Isaiah 1:1-2; 26:3; 40:29-31; Matthew 17:2; John 1:9; 6:63; 7:37; 8:12; 9:5; 14:6; Romans 6:23; 8:2; 1 Corinthians 2:16; Ephesians 4:23; Philippians 4:6-8; 1 Peter 5:7" (King, 2012)

It has been my prayer as I have written this book that it will speak life into each one who reads it. May it be a form of encouragement for you; and may you, as David, when you reach the end of this journey through the valley of the shadow of death find your cup running over with joy. Surely goodness and mercy follows you all the days of your life! Today is the first day of the rest of your life! It is a new beginning!

My Cup Runneth Over

ABOUT THE AUTHOR

Pastor Regina Sanders

Pastor Regina Sanders is a wife, mother, pastor, author, and teacher of Scripture. In January 2016 the Lord blessed her with an international satellite radio broadcast, allowing her to be heard beyond the borders of the United States. She was heard in places such as Hong Kong, Germany, and Canada. This broadcast lasted only about 4 ½ months as she was diagnosed with Stage 3 Colon Cancer in May of 2016. Pastor Regina smiles and says, "God has a sense of humor. I was teaching a group about coming out of their shell of introversion. I was writing another book on this topic, and I had this radio broadcast, as well as, my weekly YouTube uploads, and I found myself in the hospital for 11 days. Upon coming home, I found myself either in the bed or on the couch unable to continue with the tasks I had before me. Lord, you healed me of introversion, and I find myself feeling completely isolated..." Today, Pastor Regina shares her journey through the valley of the shadow of death.

CONNECT WITH ME

FACEBOOK: www.facebook.com/PastorReginaSanders
TWITTER: www.twitter.com/ReginaSanders17
BLOG: www.pastorreginasanders.blogspot.com
EMAIL: pastor.regina.sanders@gmail.com

You are VALUABLE! You are WORTHY! You are LOVED!

Made in the USA
Middletown, DE
30 March 2022

63405261R00064